PRAISE FOR SEAN DIETRICH

"Dietrich is a Southern Garrison Keillor."

—*Library Journal*

"Sean Dietrich can spin a story."

—*Southern Living*

"Sean Dietrich is Southern storytelling at its finest; reading his words is like sitting on a front porch with a Mason jar of sweet tea, listening to your uncle weave a story you know in your heart is true, but there's a little magic thrown in too."

—Annie Butterworth Jones, owner of the Bookshelf

"Southern Literature at its finest."

—*Southern Literary Review*

"Dietrich's hopeful tale [*Stars of Alabama*] illuminates the small rays of faith that shine even in dark times."

—*Publishers Weekly*

"[*Stars of Alabama* is a] big-hearted novel."

—*Garden & Gun*

"[*Stars of Alabama* is] mysterious and dazzling."

—*Deep South Magazine*

WILL THE CIRCLE BE UNBROKEN?

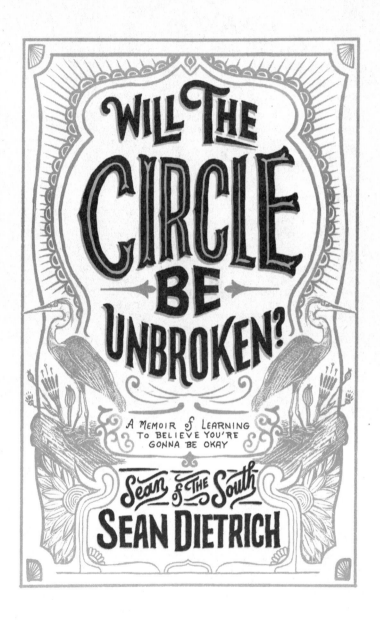

WILL THE CIRCLE BE UNBROKEN?

A MEMOIR OF LEARNING TO BELIEVE YOU'RE GONNA BE OKAY

Sean of the South

SEAN DIETRICH

ZONDERVAN BOOKS

ZONDERVAN BOOKS

Will the Circle Be Unbroken?
Copyright © 2020 by Sean Dietrich

Requests for information should be addressed to:
Zondervan, *3900 Sparks Dr. SE, Grand Rapids, Michigan 49546*

Zondervan titles may be purchased in bulk for educational, business, fundraising, or promotional use. For information, please email SpecialMarkets@Zondervan.com.

ISBN 978-0-310-35577-9 (audio)

Library of Congress Cataloging-in-Publication Data

Names: Dietrich, Sean, 1982- author.
Title: Will the circle be unbroken : a memoir of learning to believe you're gonna be okay / Sean of the South, Sean Dietrich.
Description: Grand Rapids : Zondervan, 2020. | Summary: "'Sean of the South' Sean Dietrich is known for his stories of steel workers, small towns and trusty bloodhounds, but most of all, the small, everyday evidences of true good in the world. Will the Circle Be Unbroken? is his story - told for the first time - of love, loss, and the unlikely hope that we're gonna be alright"— Provided by publisher.
Identifiers: LCCN 2019034824 (print) | LCCN 2019034825 (ebook) | ISBN 9780310355755 (hardcover) | ISBN 9780310355762 (ebook)
Subjects: LCSH: Dietrich, Sean, 1982- | Dietrich, Sean, 1982—Family. | Authors—United States—Biography. | Journalists—United States—Biography. | Bloggers—United States—Biography.
Classification: LCC PS3604.I2254 Z46 2020 (print) | LCC PS3604.I2254 (ebook) | DDC 813/.6—dc23
LC record available at https://lccn.loc.gov/2019034824
LC ebook record available at https://lccn.loc.gov/2019034825

Any internet addresses (websites, blogs, etc.) and telephone numbers in this book are offered as a resource. They are not intended in any way to be or imply an endorsement by Zondervan, nor does Zondervan vouch for the content of these sites and numbers for the life of this book.

Some of the names and identifying details have been changed to protect the privacy of individuals.

Published in association with The Bindery Agency, www.TheBinderyAgency.com.

Cover illustration: Conrad Garner / agencyrush.com
Author photo: Sean Murphy
Interior design: Denise Froehlich

Printed in the United States of America

---

23 24 25 26 27 LBC 7 6 5 4 3

TO MY MOTHER, MY WIFE, MY SISTER, AND
ELLIE MAE, THE WOMEN IN MY LIFE

CONTENTS

CHAPTER 1

CAMP CREEK

The day before my father shot himself, I saw a blue heron. I was standing on the muddy banks of Camp Creek. The bird was there for the same reason I was. We were fishing.

I was a child, standing onshore with a rod and cork float. The bird was taller than I was, with shocking eyes. He stood upright, perched on a fallen spruce that was half in the water.

The elegant bird looked straight at me. He was the picture of mystery, with his shaggy feathers, his S-shaped neck, his slender beak.

My father had always reminded me of a heron. Once, I told my father and it seemed to amuse him.

"No way," he said. "I'm not as ugly as a heron."

My father wasn't ugly, but he was lanky and birdlike. His long legs, his lean neck, his beak nose. My father's arms hung below his knees, almost like wings. And when he walked, it was with a forward lean, like he was keeping his center of gravity in the right place.

His build suited him. He was a welder, an ironworker, and birdlike qualities came in handy on the iron. He could crawl upon the skeletons of skyscrapers like a tightrope walker.

Only a few days earlier, I had watched him climb a fifty-foot tree to hang a tire swing. He did that just for me. He risked his life to do it. I'd never seen anyone climb a tree that high and live to talk about it.

"Be careful!" I yelled from the ground.

"Careful?" he said. "This ain't nothing! On a jobsite, I climb thirty stories sometimes!"

My father scaled a mostly limbless tree like a native, barefoot, jeans rolled around his ankles. Then he walked along the branch, arms spread outward for balance, a two-inch-thick rope over his shoulder.

Finally, he draped the rope over a sturdy limb and tied a bowline knot. The swing was exquisite. On his downward descent, the bark cut his forearms so that he was bleeding. But he didn't even feel it. Ironworkers are like that. He only fastened a tire to the other end of the rope, and that, by God, was that.

I burned up entire days on that swing. On it, I was a fighter pilot, a trapeze artist, a sailor of the high seas, a cowboy riding his faithful horse. To a boy who lives a hundred miles from town, a good tire swing is everything.

It's funny what you remember. There are entire years of my life that blend into beige mush, and I can hardly remember what I had for supper last night. But I remember that swing. I remember the rough, orange-and-white rope that left blisters on my hands. I remember the smell of that tire, warm and soft from the sun. I remember the way it'd be full of water after a rain, and I remember the hole I punched into the bottom of the tire with a pocketknife to prevent this.

Sometimes I remember too much.

The heron stepped carefully along the branches with perfect balance. Then he leapt onto the shore so that he was only feet away from me. He took a few steps in my direction, through the mud, leaving a trail of footprints.

Then, for no apparent reason, he stopped.

The bird gave me a hard glare. He was so still I could see a pulse throbbing in his breast. Maybe he was begging. Herons are known to beg for fish. A lot of fishermen feed them, but you weren't supposed to toss a fish to a heron. At least that's what my father told me once.

"You hungry?" I asked the bird in a quiet voice. "I'll feed you, boy."

It didn't matter what my father had told me about feeding herons. My mother taught me to always share with company.

With one hand, I reached into a brown paper bag, careful not to make much commotion. I didn't want to scare the bird. I unwrapped a sandwich of white bread, ham, and mayonnaise.

"How 'bout this?" I said. "Do you like ham, boy?"

The bird didn't answer.

"It's good. Tastes just like . . . ham."

I removed the meat from the sandwich and tossed it toward him. The thick chunk of honey-glazed ham fell several yards before the bird with a slapping against the ground. The noise spooked him. He leapt backward and resumed his perch on the limb and kept his eyes on me.

The ham was covered in sand and dirt.

"Thanks a lot," I said, biting into my all-bread sandwich. "Dumb bird."

In this memory, I was happy. Not just in part, but fully. I can see that happy child in my memory. The sun is upon his freckled skin, and he is glad, there on the banks of Camp Creek.

The child has no idea that in twenty-four hours, within the little town of Parkville, Missouri, his father will place the barrel of a hunting rifle into his mouth and alter the course of the boy's life.

This child knows nothing about the gunshot that will tear a hole in his uncle's roof, ringing throughout Parkville like the sound of a single clap, scaring birds away for miles.

The boy doesn't know that neighbors nearby will hear gunfire or that people will come running to see what happened. That sirens will whine, that police will barricade the scene with yellow tape, or that the entire world will fall.

The child is clueless. But in a few hours, once he finishes fishing, the tributary of his family stream will change, like a river that starts flowing sideways. The boy's family current will flow far away from this place, trickling downward through the Ozarks, past Mississippi, through Alabama, stopping briefly in Georgia, and finally dumping into the Florida Panhandle.

The boy knows nothing about this. Today he only knows the glories of floating corks and the taste of Sunbeam bread. These will be the last few minutes before the winter of his life. And perhaps that's why I remember them so vividly.

My fishing rod bent. My reel screamed. I cranked the fish inward only to find that it was a small catfish. It was shiny and gray. I removed the hook and was startled by the sound of loud flapping behind me. I was so startled I stabbed the hook into my hand.

The flapping was like the noise of my mother shaking a bedsheet.

When I looked, I saw the heron leaving. I saw his ascent. He flew straight overhead and climbed above the tree line. He had something in his mouth, but I couldn't tell what. His shape moved against the blue-and-white sky, heading for who knows where. His wings were wide, and his spindled legs trailed behind him like an afterthought. My God, he was something.

I turned to see that the ham was gone.

In a few hours, my father would be too.

CHAPTER 2

PAPER PLATES

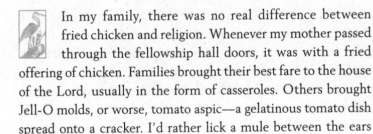

In my family, there was no real difference between fried chicken and religion. Whenever my mother passed through the fellowship hall doors, it was with a fried offering of chicken. Families brought their best fare to the house of the Lord, usually in the form of casseroles. Others brought Jell-O molds, or worse, tomato aspic—a gelatinous tomato dish spread onto a cracker. I'd rather lick a mule between the ears than eat tomato aspic.

My mother, however, always brought fried chicken. Dishes were laid upon the Blessed Altar of Folding Card Tables and blessed by the high priest.

Amen. Hallelujah. Let's eat.

I come from fundamentalist people. I came to believe those dishes were sacred. And I don't mean figuratively. I mean that when I taste good chicken, I feel warmth inside.

Long ago, my Sunday school teacher Miss Ross once explained the story of the Israelites at Passover. She told us the children of Israel would sacrifice lambs unto the Lord for the forgiveness of sins and then eat the lamb's meat. Afterward, she smiled and said to the class, "Now, can anyone tell me why we don't sacrifice lambs anymore?"

My cousin Ed Lee raised his hand and said, "Because Jesus gave us chickens instead."

"Glory!" I shouted.

"Yes, Lord!" shouted Andrew Simms, who could eat more fried chicken than most grown men.

Fried chicken fellowships were important events. They were every bit as important as Sunday services. If you were raised the way I was, you are nodding your head right now. Why else would the Southern Baptist Convention go to the trouble of building a special room dedicated to eating?

The sanctuary was for shouting. The fellowship hall was for fried foods and overcooked vegetables.

The routines of our Sunday mornings were done with the same reverence as the pageantry of a covered-dish supper. A church lady holds her post in the kitchen with the same sincerity as the music minister leading a Christmas cantata.

To my mother, scrubbing dishes in the fellowship hall sink was every bit as important as any job in the church. Just like helping my father unfold chairs was just as important to a solid Christian upbringing as memorizing the lyrics to the "Doxology."

These were our sacraments.

I grew up believing that fried chicken was a holy dish, and chickens were fundamentalist birds placed on earth to be fried for the forgiveness of sins. I didn't know whether heathens ate chickens, but I prayed they would. After all, no sinner could live in darkness after taking one bite of Miss Carolyn Williams's thick-battered short thighs.

Just one bite of my mother's chicken could bring a perishing soul back from the edge of hell and cause them to repent of a wicked lifestyle of alcoholism and substance abuse that ultimately leads to dancing.

The greatest memories of my life took place in a fellowship hall. I have no better images in my mind than these.

This was a place where elderly deacons in polyester suits flung neckties over their shoulders and had brazen love affairs with saturated fat, where stately women who smelled like Estee Lauder's Youth Dew doled out slices of apple pie with cheese on top, served on scalloped paper plates.

It was here.

When I close my eyes, I can still see the room itself. The linoleum floors, the drinking fountain, the water stain on the asbestos ceiling above the kitchen, the buffet tables, the CorningWare dishes, the spinet piano by the window used for choir practice, the bathroom no bigger than a water-heater closet, and most of all, the people. Simple people, with simple ideas, who do not believe in too much ambition.

This is where I discovered who I am. This is where I first learned that I was a rural person. In my life, I have lived many places and been many things. My father was a steelworker, and we bounced between cities and states like a pinball so that I never seemed to know where I belonged.

If the Mason-Dixon Line extended west, I was born 1,126 feet from its border, on the southern side, in Missouri. My father told me that made me a Southerner by birth—just barely. My family ancestry was divided. Some fought in the Confederate Army. Some for the Union. They say that my great-great-grandfather Eustis G. Seetin almost lost his right foot in the First Battle of Lexington as a Confederate soldier, and he was so peeved about it that he switched sides and fought for the Union. I don't know what that makes me.

What I can tell you is that my father was a Kansan, my mother made me a Southerner, and sometimes I wonder who I am.

Still, no matter where we found ourselves, I was at home in a fellowship hall.

It was here that I felt the glow of a hearth. The preacher

would holler a blessing over the food, shouting loud enough for all forty-three church members to hear, using the trademarked voice of fundamentalists: a voice that carried a lot of authority and a little agitation. He would speak in an ancient Baptist rhythm that men quit using long ago. And we, the redeemed of the Lord, would fold our hands, clench our eyelids, and this was home.

During these moments of prayer, the smell of cooked chicken would drift into my nostrils, and forevermore religion and poultry became married in my mind. Eternal security and fried gizzards. Hymns and ham. Prayers and pound cake. Singing and sweet tea. I could do this all day.

Once, my friend James invited me to his house for supper. His family was from Pennsylvania. I had never met anyone from Pennsylvania. They were a happy family, with strange accents. It was a treat to hear his parents use the words "you guys" instead of "y'all" and refer to Coca-Cola as "soady pop."

That night for supper, my friend's mother served baked chicken breasts with pineapple slices and cherries.

I had never seen chicken cooked this way. The dish looked like something from a science-fiction movie, minus the tentacles. I stabbed the breast with my fork. It was so dry you could've used it to sand oil stains off the driveway.

I whispered to my friend, "Hey, what's wrong with this chicken?"

"What do you mean?" he said.

"It's not fried."

"Oh," he said. "We don't fry chicken. We're Catholic."

And I felt sorry for my friend. I didn't want him to perish in a life of alien dry chicken. That same week, I invited my friend to a Wednesday night potluck. We walked through the line together. When we reached my mother's fried chicken, I placed two drumsticks on my friend's plate and offered no further instruction.

My friend sat at the table beside me. When he lifted a drumstick to his mouth, I saw his eyes glow with the Light of Salvation.

Today, my friend is a Southern Baptist minister.

No fundamentalist could have loved fried chicken more than my father. And he's what this book is about, so I suppose I ought to introduce you to him.

Besides steelwork, my father only considered two things in this world worthy of his time. Fried chicken and baseball. I remember when he called in sick for work, simply because he didn't want to miss the sixth game of the World Series between the Saint Louis Cardinals and the Kansas City Royals. He got so excited when Kansas City won the series that he walked outside and fired a shotgun into the air. And I remember the way he ate. Without reserve. I remember how he would remove his sport coat, toss his necktie over his shoulder, take a bite, and let out a moan. Always he would moan. It was ritual.

Because I wanted to be just like my father, I did the same. I rolled up my sleeves, tossed my tie over my shoulder, took a bite, and moaned. Together we would have grease on our faces and shiny fingers.

Then my father would grin at me, as if to say, "Ain't it good?" But he wouldn't actually say it because his mouth was full.

I can still see that smile in my dreams.

I was not yet twelve when my father removed himself from this world. It had been shaping up to be a good year, but it would never be. My father offed himself in Missouri with a hunting rifle. And the winter of our lives began.

The Saturday night before his funeral, a small crowd gathered in a fellowship hall. People wore solemn faces and black clothes. Miss Carolyn made fried chicken.

It was a strange night. I couldn't speak, let alone eat. Whenever anyone talked to me, I could only look at their mouths and watch their lips move. But I could not hear them. I was too stunned to remember my own name.

But the room was not solemn. It was filled with people who ate chicken, laughed, tossed their plates into the garbage, refilled their tea, and went back to the buffet for seconds.

It was too much for me. I couldn't understand how anyone could eat when my father had just participated in a homicide in which he was both the victim and the criminal.

So I went into the tiny bathroom and cried with the faucet running so nobody could hear me. I didn't want to go back home to our farmhouse. I wanted to stay in that room, in that blessed hall, and make a new life there. I never wanted to leave it. And one day, perhaps, when my appetite came back, maybe there would even be chicken waiting for me.

After an hour, there was a knock on the door. It was a gentle knock.

"Go away," I said.

Another knock.

"Leave me alone!" I shouted. I was crying pretty hard.

"Please come out," said my mother. "Please, you're worrying me."

"I said go away!"

Knock, knock, knock.

I cussed. And all these years later, I'm still sorry I did.

The knocking stopped. It was another hour before I finally emerged. By then, the sounds of the crowd in the fellowship hall had died. People had left to go resume their normal, happy lives and left my family to flop in the dirt like dying fish.

I opened the door to see an old man and woman, sitting in folding chairs facing the bathroom door, waiting.

I wiped my face. I had a headache. Two hours of crying dehydrates a body.

The elderly people were the only ones left in the room, and

I'll never forget them. He was bald, wearing dark glasses, holding a white cane. The woman wore a beehive hairdo and denim skirt. These were country people. I could tell by the way they dressed. I come from this brand of people. I can pick them out of a crowd. I'd never met them before.

The blind man was smiling, though not looking in my direction. His sunglasses were aimed above me.

"Is that him?" he asked the old woman.

"Yes," she said. "He's finally come out."

"Oh, good," he said.

The man stood. He walked toward me with cautious steps. He reached his hand outward until he found my shoulder. Then he knelt to my eye-level. It hurt him to do it. I could hear him grunting beneath his own weight.

He smiled again. And in a drawl thick enough to pave county roads, he said, "I want you to listen to me, son."

I said nothing.

The old man hugged me. It was a firm embrace. The kind that grandparents give to grandchildren. "You're gonna be alright," he said.

He smelled like sweat and Old Spice. He was still holding on. It was one of the first hugs I'd allowed after my father pulled the trigger.

"You hear me?" he said. "You're gonna be *allll riiight.*"

I could not bring myself to answer him because I wasn't sure I believed him.

Finally, the old woman helped him to his feet, and they shuffled out of the fellowship hall like two spirits, rejoining the clouds from whence they came.

And my mother appeared with a horde of women who tackled me. They kissed me, cried on me, and squeezed me until my ribs hurt.

I asked my mother who the blind man was.

"What blind man?" she said.

"The man who just left."

"I didn't see anyone, sweetie."

And I wanted to follow him. I wanted to ask this man how he knew my family, or if he had known my father. I wanted to ask if my father ever talked about me or said good things about the way I played first base. I wanted to know where he got the gall to say what he said. But he was gone before I could, and it had already started gnawing at me.

Then six women tried to smother me to death with lipstick and flabby arms.

My childhood was not a pretty one, but I believe ugly child-hoods make pretty people. I have gone through moments when I doubted the things I thought I knew. I've experienced tragedy like anyone else. I've lost people, I've buried good dogs, I've been uncertain where I belong, I've been a Kansan, and I've been a Southerner. I've been a loser and man who feels like he won life's lottery. But no matter where life takes me, I will always be a rural child and a survivor of suicide.

I am like anyone else who gathers in a fellowship hall. I've endured sadness, horror, grief, anxiety, and football teams who just can't seem to win a national championship. I've lived through dark decades when the sun wouldn't show itself. But when I walk into any fellowship hall in the USA on a Wednesday night, bad things go away. You can always visit a fellowship hall to see and feel the same things.

You pass through the doors. Miss Carolyn Williams sees you. She makes a beeline for you and hugs your neck. She is still wearing her apron. She has an oily forehead. She smells like a kitchen.

You load your flimsy scalloped paper plate to capacity. You find a seat next to people you know. Before you eat, a preacher says grace in a loud, sing-songy voice.

"Bless this food, Lord," he bellows. "And bless the hands that prepared it . . ."

They always bless the hands.

And it is in this room that you are swept away in the current of your ancestors who fought on both sides of the Mason-Dixon Line before observing peace. You can't see them, but their ghosts are still here. They are grinning at you.

These are *their* folding tables. These people are *their* offspring, who are retelling *their* stories. *They* built this place. And these people know you, just like they knew your parents. They remember you when you were a wayward young man. They even prayed for you, though you didn't know it.

They are deacons, farmers, millworkers, lawyers, steelworkers, elders, insurance salesmen, janitors, doctors, cooks, bartenders, and carpenters. Strong men, rural men, dignified men who aren't afraid to lick their fingers when they eat chicken.

In these halls, children chase one another through the maze of folding chairs. Ladies catch up on gossip, whispering. Preachers engage in their only permissible vice, refined sugar. And within this room, you are brought back to the middle again.

You start remembering good things instead of bad. You glance at the stain on the ceiling, and you recall your Catholic friend whose mother made chicken that tasted like goat pellets.

You close your eyes and see the image of your mother holding a covered dish. You feel the memory of your father, the most confusing man you ever knew, who ruined your life but also made your life what it is. A tapestry of things both reprehensible and exquisite. A man who once sat beside you with a necktie flung over his shoulder. Who loved you.

You wonder how this beautiful person had the audacity to leave all this behind.

And you are forever haunted by fellowship halls, even when you aren't in them. You dream of them. You can't wait to revisit them. They are your proof. Evidence that life is not against you. A reminder that eventually, no matter what it seems like, the tables will be set up, folding chairs will be unfolded, tablecloths will be unfurled, casseroles will arrive by the thousands. You will eat the food of your people. The homemade biscuits, the tea with too much sugar, and the fried chicken. And it will hit you all at once. No matter how bad it looks, that blind man was telling the truth.

Everything will be alright.

CHAPTER 3

CASKETS

 Southeastern Kansas was nothing but sunshine. My father's visitation fell on a September day beautiful enough to make your heart hurt. The birds were singing. The sky was blue. This weather was all wrong.

I wanted foreboding clouds, hailstorms, tornadoes, hurricanes, tsunamis, maybe a decent earthquake. They would have suited the day much better. Instead, we had weather fit for a picnic.

We spent the afternoon at a small funeral home, a god-awful place on the edge of town, owned and operated by a man who wore a hairpiece that didn't match the gray on the sides of his head.

I shook hands with a long line of visitors who were all crying harder than I was. It felt strange. I was a foreigner among them. I stood next to my mother. She was small and lean. She wasn't crying. Only a few days earlier, my father had tried to take her out of this world.

My four-year-old sister was with my aunt near an empty casket, lying on her stomach, coloring in a coloring book, singing to herself, her blond curls hanging over her eyes.

The visitors were from all walks of life but mostly country people who all pronounced *Lord* as *Lowered* and *Jesus* as *Jeez's*.

They said things about my father that were meant to make me feel warm and fuzzy. They told anecdotes that bordered on legendary. Most tales were meant to make me appreciate my father instead of remembering his last horrific night.

Besides, people don't say average things about dead men. They say incredible things, turn his minor triumphs into astonishing feats, and make him sound like a bona fide saint.

My father was no saint.

Finally, when I'd had enough hand-shaking, I snuck away and wandered a long hallway through a crowd who wore drab colors and too much perfume. They all wanted to tousle my hair, kiss my forehead, or hug me until my eyes bulged.

I chose a door at random. It led into a room that was dark and quiet and very cold, like a giant refrigerator.

Finally, I was alone, away from aunts who smeared flesh-colored makeup on my cheeks and told me how tall I was getting. I needed space to think.

This room was covered in a paper-thin film of frost. I could see my breath like steam. Then I saw it. Before me, I saw bare feet poking from beneath a white sheet. A paper tag was tied around one of the toes like the tag on Minnie Pearl's hat.

I shrieked.

It was a woman's toe. At least, I *think* it was a woman. I didn't have the guts to ask her. I started to tremble. The whole room was full of the deceased, and it smelled of mint, disinfectant, and something else I couldn't identify. I wondered if my father was in this room. I started to feel sick. But I couldn't make myself leave.

Earlier that week, I'd heard the police talking to my mother on the front porch.

"We had to use dental records to identify him . . ." said one deputy, hat in hand. "He was a real mess."

Those words will never leave me. My father had inserted the

barrel of a rifle into his mouth and pulled the trigger with his toes. All that remained were his teeth.

I curled in a chair. I was not the sort of kid who could handle horrific things. I had never even seen a movie with blood in it. I was raised by Baptists who had moderate curiosity in speaking in tongues. They were people who didn't smoke, drink, chew, or listen to Conway Twitty in public. Their children did not watch movies unless they were animated features about elephants who could fly. Any film depicting monsters, gore, the occult, or flagrant Episcopalianism was strictly forbidden.

At Halloween, my mother would only allow me to dress up as nonhorror characters. Thus, I was the only kid among my peers who went trick-or-treating as an angel or Moses or Oral Roberts, and one year—I'm not making this up—I went as Jesus.

Being Jesus was my mother's idea. She'd dressed me in her white bathrobe and then placed a Christmas wreath on my head to represent the crown of thorns. Before my mother sent me off, she kissed my forehead and almost started crying. "Oh, look at you," she said. "Mama's little Redeemer."

When I visited Mister Wallace's doorstep, he took one look at me and said, "Well, well, if it isn't the Ghost of Christmas Present."

"No sir," I pointed out. "I'm Jesus."

"Who?"

"The Fairest of Ten Thousand."

"For Halloween?"

"Yessir."

"Why haven't you said 'trick or treat'?"

"I'm not here for tricks, sir. I'm here to offer forgiveness." And I held my pillow case outward.

He tossed eighteen dollars into my sack and said, "That's all you get. I already gave last Sunday."

Something in me had to touch the body. I don't know why. I

stepped toward the corpse. I rested my hand on the ankle. It was cold. I almost started crying, but I couldn't seem to make tears.

I was not ready for death. In fact, I had only seen dead people exactly three times in my life. Once, when Granny died. Once, when Granddaddy died. And once, when my friend Lena's mother died.

Lena's mother was the worst of the three because she was killed in her prime. She was a lovely young woman with a shock of red hair. She commanded the attention of all the males in church.

Once, Lena's mother attended a high school baseball game. They say all the boys in the outfield found it nearly impossible to concentrate on flying baseballs. There were three concussions reported after that game.

Only a week before Lena's mother died, she had made sugar cookies for us. She'd told jokes and given us rides into town, driving her husband's truck. She'd smoked cigarettes while guarding the playground for Vacation Bible School. She taught us to sing "Jesus Loves Me," and she was a painter. She died one summer night from an allergic reaction to bees. My friend Lena was nine.

I'll never forget the way Lena looked on the night of her mother's funeral. I attended the visitation with my father. He and I waited in the receiving line wearing neckties, heads bowed. It was open casket. Lena's mother was lying with arms folded across her chest and a phony look of rest frozen on her face. Her red hair was fixed pretty.

Lena was a zombie. I'd never seen her so calm.

Lena was a tomboy who could beat me at arm wrestling, leg wrestling, or even thumb wrestling. She was the girl who could level any boy with one punch to the jaw. A girl who could gut a largemouth bass and chew more Red Man than any hick in the county. She was the first girl I ever kissed. We were first graders at the time, and she tasted like Nehi soda because that's what she'd been drinking. After she kissed me, she punched me in the stomach to remind me who was boss. Marriage, I would discover years later, is not all that different.

She became an orphan overnight.

The day of her mother's service, I expected Lena to collapse in tears, but she didn't. She was the ghost of someone I knew. Even more strange, she was wearing a lace dress. I'd never seen her in anything but denim and T-shirts.

When I saw her in that receiving line, she asked, "Do you like my makeup?"

I thought it was a bizarre question.

"Yeah," I said.

"My sister did it." She gave me a hard look. "Do you *really* like it? Hand to God?"

"Hand to God."

"It was my mother's lipstick."

"You look nice."

"These earrings were Mama's too. Do you like them?"

"Yeah."

"Hand to God?"

"If I'm lying, I'm dying."

"I had to get my ears pierced. Christy did it with a needle and ice cube last night. I didn't even bleed. Isn't that something? Everyone bleeds, but I didn't."

"That's really something, Lena."

"I know. I thought I would bleed."

That's when her eyes got wet.

I wanted to take her away and make the world go back to normal. But all I could do was hug her. The dam inside her broke, and she cried into my shoulder and ruined my sport coat with saltwater.

After her mother's funeral, my father took me to a drive-in

restaurant. We ate chili dogs, sitting on his tailgate, neckties loosened. Neither of us spoke. Losing a young person makes everyone think sober thoughts.

I stared at the skinny man beside me. He had a long neck, spindled legs, and arms like wings. He looked like he could leap off that truck bed and start flying upward into the night sky if he'd wanted. I was afraid. If Lena's mother had left her, that meant that my father could leave me. I didn't want him to leave. I wanted to hold onto him forever. I wanted him to stay for a very long time.

But you can't control birds. They are untamed and skittish. If they get spooked, they're off to heaven with no worry about you. They do what they want.

The door opened and a beam of light shot across the floor. I saw a shadowy figure in the doorway. It was a girl. She was my age. A tomboy, wearing lace, hair in ribbons.

"Hey," Lena whispered. "What're you doing in here? Everyone's going crazy looking for you. Your mama's worried half to death."

I said nothing.

She walked toward me. "My, my," she said, straightening my collar. "Look at you, all dressed up. You look good enough to take to a meeting."

The necktie had belonged to my late father. The sport coat too. And his eyeglasses—though I have perfect vision.

"I didn't know you wore glasses," she said.

"Do you like 'em?" I asked.

"Sure."

"Hand to God?"

And Lena let me ruin the shoulder of her dress.

CHAPTER 4

CARDBOARD BOXES

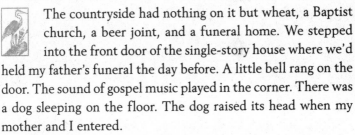The countryside had nothing on it but wheat, a Baptist church, a beer joint, and a funeral home. We stepped into the front door of the single-story house where we'd held my father's funeral the day before. A little bell rang on the door. The sound of gospel music played in the corner. There was a dog sleeping on the floor. The dog raised its head when my mother and I entered.

The woman behind the counter wore plaid and smoked a cigarette. She was reading a magazine, tapping her ashes into a saucer that sat beside a cardboard box—my father's eternal home.

There was a label on my father's container.

"Contents fragile."

Was this a joke? What could be fragile about ashes? Ashes are the least fragile state of being there is. Ashes are what things become when they are no longer fragile.

That's when it hit me. All my life, my father had been anything but fragile. He was loud, funny, and able to leap tall buildings. He'd been my childhood hero and everything I wanted to be. He was a cross between a Roy Rogers and Mickey Mantle. If you placed a cowboy hat on his head and a baseball bat in his hand, you would've seen what I mean.

Now he was a UPS parcel.

"This is him?" I asked the woman.

She lowered her magazine. "No, baby. This is only a box, your father is with *Jeez's*. He's free as a bird now." She said it like she'd said that a few times before.

"Free?" I said.

"*Free at last, free at last*," she said, touching a fresh cigarette to her diminishing one. "Careful when you lift him. That box is heavier than it looks."

I scooped it into my arms. The woman was right. Daddy was too heavy to manage. I lost control and dropped it. He hit the floor and tumbled onto his side. It sounded like I'd dropped a bowling ball on the wood planks of the funeral home.

I felt so badly I almost lost consciousness. I stooped to pick him up, but I started to melt. The whole week of funerals and funeral food was catching up with me. He was gone. Nothing I could do would ever get him out of this box.

My mother rushed to me and wrapped her arms around me.

The first feelings of bitterness I would ever feel toward my father rose within me. There, on the floor of the funeral home, I realized my father was no hero, and never had been. Neither Roy Rogers nor Mickey Mantle. He was a man who had a county mugshot taken in the Leavenworth County jailhouse a few hours before he died.

"How could he?" I said to my mother. Or maybe I wasn't saying it to her. Maybe I was saying it to the dog.

The woman from behind the counter came to me. She stroked my hair. "Remember the good times," said the woman.

I looked at her. I was getting angry. This was a stranger. What did she know about "good times"? All she had to do was look at my mother, whose eye was black, whose lip was busted. There were stitches in my mother's legs and his handprints around her neck.

"I hate him!" I shouted. Then I called him an ugly word that isn't worth repeating.

The woman behind the counter said, "Don't use language like that. The *Lowered* don't like coarse talk."

My mother took my face in both hands. She was so young, with brown curly hair that never seemed to do what she wanted it to. Her eyes filled with water. I thought she was going to slap me, but she didn't. "I don't ever wanna hear you say that again, you hear me? Never."

"It's true!" I said, and I called him the worst name I could think of.

She slapped me.

I was embarrassed. I closed my eyes. I wished it were me in that box. I wished I had been turned into soot. Instead I was alive, and sad. I was made of fragile muscle and thin blood.

"Try to remember the good in him, son," the woman said.

My mother shook my shoulders. "I will *not* have my son turning into a bitter man, do you hear me?" She gripped my chin. "Now pick up your father."

I made no moves to lift him.

"I said pick him up," she told me. "Right now."

I lifted his box into my arms. I had to hold him against my chest.

The label read: "John Dietrich." It was not just his name. It was my name too. *Dietrich* was me. He gave that name to me. He left a part of himself behind.

On the ride home, I tried to remember something good like the woman in the funeral home suggested. While the peanut fields, soy, and alfalfa passed by our windows, I fell asleep with my father on my lap.

I remembered the family reunion in Humboldt—a three-hundred-person town of my father's birth. It was *his* town. A place so small that both city-limit signs were mounted on the same post.

My father was young in my dream. And lean. Tall, with strong features, and humble to a fault. He carried a baseball bat in one hand and a beer in the other. He rarely drank in public because fundamentalist men did not do this. But in Humboldt, he was what he was.

There were other men on the baseball field that day. They were men like him. They were hard workers, and powerful. Each of them sipping from cans.

I knew them. They were men who planted wheat, corn, and soy. They were concrete mill workers, stick welders, live-stock people, and pipefitters. People who were weighted with the chains of daily labor and knew nothing else. Men whose purification came by work. The forgiveness of sins, by sweat.

They were men who hunted, but not for fun. Men who used belts on their children and hugged them hard when the licking was done. Men who laid beneath their own vehicles on week-nights and drained the belly pans of their Fords. Men who were bound by obligation to family and friends, and who were never truly free—not even on weekends.

My father handed me his beer. "Hold this," he said. "I gotta warm up my arm." My father flung his right arm in circles. He rotated his head.

"What're you doing?" I asked.

"Loosening up," he said.

"Why?"

"Don't wanna strain a muscle. Pitchers get the most injuries, you know."

"Were you a pitcher?"

"Sorta. When I was a young'un, I wanted to be the next Walter Johnson."

"Who's that?"

My father stopped stretching. "You don't know who *Walter Johnson* is? What dipstick raised you?"

He was talking about the famed pioneer of the sidearm fastball. Humboldt was Walter's hometown. Here he was a god.

"Why, he was the greatest pitcher to ever play the game," said my father. "And that's no opinion, that's what Ty Cobb said. And you *know* who Ty Cobb is, don't you?"

"Of course, his picture is on the wall in your closet."

"Good boy."

My father removed his shirt to reveal freckled skin peppered with auburn chest hair. His forearms were dark gold, his neck was brick red, and his torso was blinding white and puny.

The men formed teams. Shirts against skins. They gathered around a truck hood and bantered about the finer points of the game, laughing.

My father assumed control of the mound. And in his face, I saw a man who became three hundred years younger. He was no longer blue-collar, or a father, or a man obligated to serve as usher at the church. He was the lanky high schooler who looked almost birdlike, who everybody in town thought showed promise. You could practically hear the old men in town chatting about him in the hardware store, talking about the incredible things this teenager would do one day. Things he would never do.

But on this mound, his past disappeared, and he was once again a fella who could sure enough throw.

I had once seen my father pitch through a moving tire swing from ninety feet away.

I sat on the hood of his truck, idolizing him.

I overheard one onlooker on the bleachers. It was an old man in suspenders, sipping from a can, balancing it on his round belly. He said, "Why, that's John Dietrich. My God, haven't seen him in years."

"My, my," said another. "He looks just like his daddy, don't he?"

"Sorta, only skinnier."

"Well, not everyone can be as well-built as you are."

"It's a curse more than a gift."

Daddy pitched like I'd never seen. The ball moved so fast you could hear it cut the air in half. It smacked the catcher's mitt with the marvelous sound that gives a boy's life value.

But my father didn't break a smile. He was all business. He only did it again. And again. Each pitch hit the catcher's glove so hard the poor man had to take a minute to give his hand some air.

My father's long limbs were graceful; his face was easy. His legs were so long they bent in three places. When he'd wind up, he'd hike a knee upward to his nose, then kick his size-thirteen shoe outward, and pitch around his own foot.

"C'mon, John!" hollered the catcher. "Throw the heat!"

The wind up.

The pitch.

Strike.

"Is that John Dietrich?" shouted another old man in the stands. "Or is that Walter Perry Johnson?"

I will remember that particular day forever, because you don't forget your heroes. Not even the ones who fail you.

When we arrived home that night, the famed baseball hero was nothing but a parcel. My aunt told me to put his ashes in the barn because it was bad luck to keep the dead in the house once they'd been freed.

So I placed his box on a shelf in the barn. I sat in the corner and watched his box for nearly an hour. I was confused. I hated him, but I felt bad about hating him too.

Before I finally left, I rested a hand on his box. "I'm sorry I called you that name, Daddy."

He didn't answer. And why should he? He was soaring upward, without ties to our world. Free. That's what he was. My father was free at last.

We left Kansas forever so that we could be too.

CHAPTER 5

"ROSE COLORED GLASSES"

 We stayed with my aunt and uncle in Jonesboro, Georgia, in their upstairs bedroom over the garage. When my uncle left for work early in the morning, he opened the electric garage door beneath us, and it rumbled the bedroom hard enough to vibrate pictures off the walls.

My aunt's house smelled funny, which she was always blaming on my uncle. And almost every night, my mother and aunt would stay up, talking until the wee hours. Sometimes I could hear their hushed voices through the heating vents. My mother never spoke ill of my father, even though he'd tried to carry her to the grave with him.

Occasionally I would stumble into the kitchen for a midnight snack—a pickle maybe, or some ham, a leftover drumstick, a hambone steak sandwich with extra mayo—and my mother would stop talking. She would wait for me to leave.

I was unwelcome in her private conversations. And I knew why. They were always about him.

In this brief period of time, his name was erased from our lives. We did not talk about my father openly, nor did we talk about him privately. There were no pictures of him, and there were no funny stories told.

My mother never mentioned Kansas, and I started to forget all about the steelworker who left us. My own past started to leave me, and it was as though I had been born not as a baby but as a full-grown boy. Nothing existed before now. We had new names, new faces, new interests, and a new family. It was supposed to be wonderful, starting over. But it felt more like having a frontal lobotomy.

I was surrounded by a hive of strong-willed females. I had aunts and cousins everywhere, not a male among them.

Except my uncle. At suppers, I would sit next to my uncle and try to glean as much testosterone from him as I could. He was the kind of man who always picked his nose—even if people were looking right at him. He was shameless, clever, and always smelled like spinach that had gone bad. He had the social graces of a feral cat, and he taught me how to clear my throat and spit like I meant it.

He ate peanut butter with every meal. No matter what sort of food was on his supper plate, he ate peanut butter along with it.

My uncle could've had a reserved table for two at the *La Tour D'Argent* in Paris, and he still would've asked for peanut butter toast.

"Excuse me, *monsieur*," a waiter might ask. "What are we having *zis* evening?"

"Yes," my uncle would answer. "I'll have a glass of Bordeaux, the *crème de poulet*, and your finest jar of Jif, *s'il vous plaît*."

At supper, my mother would sit across from him. She didn't eat much after my father died. She lost weight in the months following his death and developed the faintest streak of gray in her hair. She had also lost her love of talking—which was unlike her. My mother had always been a talkative woman. In fact, it used to be her most noticeable attribute.

One particular night, over supper, my uncle announced:

"Everybody needs to get some sleep tonight. We're waking up early tomorrow. Got it?"

Then he dipped a spoon into a Jif jar and unloaded a wad of peanut butter onto a slice of Sunbeam bread.

"So get to bed early tonight," he went on, "or else you'll be miserable tomorrow morning."

"What's tomorrow?" I asked.

My mother and uncle exchanged a look without saying anything.

"Where are we going?" my baby sister said.

"Just get some sleep," my uncle went on. "We wanna make good time. I wanna beat the traffic."

"Making good time" was, perhaps, the most important thing to my uncle. It ranked somewhere between not driving too slow in the fast lane and standing for the National Anthem. If the good Lord himself had turned my uncle away from the pearly gates, my uncle would've fired up a Studebaker and sped toward hell just to "make good time."

My uncle once claimed that he'd made it from Florida to Atlanta in only three and a half hours. One day, I am certain, they will etch this on his tombstone.

Making good time came with a price. It meant that bathroom breaks were strongly discouraged. Instead, my uncle carried a Maxwell House can beneath his seat for dire emergencies. Nobody had ever seen it used, but rumor had it, the can was so old and rusted over that you had to get a tetanus shot before using it.

That night, I laid on the floor, sleeping beneath my mother and my sister. I stared at a popcorn ceiling, counting water stains until I fell asleep.

I heard a noise. My sister climbed off the bed and crawled into my sleeping bag beside me. She was tiny, with clammy hands and ice-cold feet.

"Where're we going tomorrow?" she whispered in my ear.

"I don't know," I said. "They don't wanna tell us."

"You don't think Mama's getting rid of us, do you?"

"No, don't be silly. Why would you say a thing like that?"

"Because I'm scared."

"About what?"

"I'm just scared."

"Don't be. I'm here."

"But what if you die one day?"

"I'm not gonna die."

"Not ever."

"Not any time soon."

"Promise?"

"Yes."

She fell asleep with her head on my chest. She was small and frail, and she snored like a Massey Ferguson tractor. I didn't fall asleep that night.

Then came a knocking sound. My uncle beat on the door like he was going to knock it down.

"C'mon," he said. "We gotta hurry if we're gonna . . ."

"I know, I know!" my mother yelled. "We gotta leave now if we wanna *make good time*. It's three in the morning!"

He beat on the door again. "Gotta hurry!"

My mother rubbed her eyes. "I'm gonna kill that son of a—"

KNOCK! KNOCK! KNOCK!

My mother screamed, "If you don't stop that beating, I'm gonna neuter you with dressmaking shears!"

The knocking stopped.

But only momentarily. In a few minutes, the door was open, and there was a man marching in our room, banging a spoon against an empty stock pot, singing the "Army Song" at the top of his lungs.

"Over hill, over dale, as we hit the dusty trail, and those caissons go rolling along . . ."

My mother threw the Atlanta Metropolitan Yellow Pages at him. He only laughed and sang louder.

I believe my uncle is mentally unstable.

We loaded our luggage into his car like the living dead, tired, yawning. I balanced my sister on my hip. She was still asleep. When the vehicle was loaded, my mother said, "Go get your father from the garage," and I knew where we were going.

"You want me to get Daddy?" I said.

"Do as I say. Your uncle's in a hurry."

I placed my sister in the backseat, walked to the garage, and retrieved my father's box. He was high up, on a shelf between a gas can and a leaf blower. I carried the heavy thing against my chest.

My uncle met me beside his trunk hatch. He touched my shoulder and said in a quiet voice, "I need you to be brave for your mother. Can you do that?"

"What do you mean?"

He squatted. "I mean that you're the man of your family now, and that means you have to be the strongest. Be brave for your mother."

I nodded, though I had no idea what it meant.

Soon we were speeding so fast the wheels almost blew off the axles and the floorboards were getting hot. My uncle sped out of the Great American South faster than Dale Earnhardt on a beer run.

My mother sat in the front seat, sleeping with her head against the window. My sister and cousin sat beside me in the backseat, curled up together. I could not sleep. I stared out the window at the stars and wondered what would become of us. The whole world was falling apart.

On the day—and I mean the actual day—of my father's death, the commissioner of baseball announced they would be canceling the World Series. The story ran on the front page the next morning. It was the first year since 1904 without a World Series.

Consequently, in the rear section of that same newspaper was news of my father's death.

It was like Armageddon. How could they cancel baseball? What was next? Easter? Thanksgiving? Would someone assassinate Santa, then sneak into his workshop, burn it to the ground, and tattoo three sixes on all the elves' foreheads?

What would happen to my favorite baseball players? Would we walk into a Piggly Wiggly and see Greg Maddux wearing a red apron, asking if we wanted help loading the car? Would Bobby Cox be on the street corner downtown, offering to wash windows for pocket change?

The world had changed overnight. And I didn't know if I would survive it. That's what I was thinking when I watched the sunrise in the rear window of my uncle's car.

That morning, somewhere near Fort Campbell, Kentucky, I felt a sensation in my bladder that posed a serious threat to my uncle's wool upholstery. I told my uncle this.

"Too bad," proclaimed my uncle. "We ain't stopping until I get outta this traffic."

"But," I said, "it's serious."

"Sorry. Gotta hurry if we're gonna make good time."

"I've been holding it since Tennessee."

"Tough."

I bounced my knees. I gritted my teeth. I began praying to the Virgin Guadalupe. But when I began hip-swiveling, I knew I had reached what is commonly known among medical professionals as "the bargaining stage."

"Please!" I shouted.

He slapped his hands on the steering wheel. "But we're making *great* time," he said. "Can't you hold it until Paducah?"

"NONO! It's coming!" I was red-lining. I had reached the point in a boy's life when he discovers the limits of his pelvic floor muscles.

My uncle tossed me an empty Maxwell House coffee can.

"Don't spill a drop," he said. "Or so help me . . ."

The can was rusted, and there was a family of horseflies who had claimed it as their primary residence.

"I can't go in this!" I shouted.

"Sure you can!" he shouted back. "People in our family have been using that can since Dwight D. Eisenhower was in office."

I turned my body for privacy and knelt on the seat with my back to my toddler cousin and sister, who were both giggling.

"You better not be making a mess back there!" my uncle hollered. "I know where you sleep!"

But something was wrong. I wasn't able to go with an audience. My urinary muscles had temporarily locked.

"I can't *go* with people watching," I said. "Can't we just pull over?"

"Too much traffic," my uncle said. "How about a little camouflage?" My uncle turned on the radio, full blast.

Through the speakers came John Conlee's anthem "Rose Colored Glasses." His voice gave me ease. I felt my muscles relax.

I have been a Conlee fan ever since.

I filled the can nearly to the top. When I finished, I handed the can to my mother, who almost socked me in the mouth.

"I don't want it!" she shouted.

So she handed it to my uncle, who nearly lost control of the vehicle.

"Are you nuts?" he yelled. "Don't give it to *me*! I don't want his . . ."

The car swerved.

"Dump it out the window," my mother said.

The events that unfolded next would live in Dietrich family folklore for generations to come, to be discussed at various family reunions, potlucks, and beer joints all over the world.

My uncle, piloting a car at eighty miles per hour on Highway 40, held the coffee can in his right hand and attempted to crank his window with his left hand. He steered with his right knee.

John Conlee was singing his encore chorus, and—so help me—time slowed down.

My uncle dumped the can out the window, but the draft was too strong. The high-velocity wind current whipped the contents backward against him, and thus he was baptized in the name of the Father, the Son, and Sean Dietrich.

We did not make good time that day.

CHAPTER 6

PIKES PEAK

After three days in my uncle's car, we arrived in Colorado Springs, and everyone's faces were glued to the windows. The snowcapped mountains in the distance looked like poetry, tall and ageless. There was something about them, something looming, almost like they'd been waiting for us.

We slept in a cheap motel. Everyone piled into two rooms. I slept between my sister and my cousin, who were violent sleepers. My cousin kicked me in the shin, and my sister was drooling on me. In the middle of the night, I decided to take my chances on the floor with the roaches and rodents.

The next morning, I awoke to find my mother standing in the breezeway of the motel. It was still dark. She was staring at the mountains. The lights of the city illuminated the faint suggestion of the Rockies in the background. I stumbled out of our room.

"What're you thinking?" I asked.

She looked at me with a lifetime of sorrow in her eyes. "Doesn't matter," she said.

"Why here?" I asked.

She gave a faint smile. "Go back to bed," she said. "You can still get another hour of sleep before breakfast."

"Aren't you gonna tell me?"

"You're gonna need your sleep. Big day today."

"Please, Mama."

She let out a sigh. "These were his wishes."

I looked into the parking lot and could see my uncle's vehicle. In the trunk was a cardboard box. I knew we would not be returning home with it.

The sun rose over the Rockies. It was enough to take your breath away. My uncle and I ate cereal on the motel steps while my sister and cousin watched cartoons at maximum volume. My mother remained in the breezeway, where she'd been most of the night.

My uncle took a bite of cereal and said with a full mouth, "From the top of Pikes Peak you can see Kansas, New Mexico, Wyoming, part of Oklahoma, and some folks even claim they can see Arkansas."

It was on this mountain my father wanted to be scattered. On the top. Everyone but me seemed to know why.

"Why did he want to be scattered here?" I asked my uncle.

My uncle shrugged. "Who cares? Your father wanted it. That's enough reason."

We piled into the car and drove to the top of the mountain. Our ears popped and our breathing became labored. We stopped at the gift shop, which lies part way up the great mountain. I stood in line to use the bathroom. A group of Japanese tourists were ahead of me, cameras dangling around their necks. I read a flyer while I waited.

I learned that Pikes Peak was the same place where one hundred years ago a woman named Katharine Lee Bates once became so inspired she wrote a song about "amber waves of grain" and "purple mountains majesties." It turned out to be a big hit.

After I exited the bathroom, a Japanese woman asked if

I would take a picture of her family. Everyone posed before a guardrail and did not smile. I noticed this when I looked into the viewfinder.

"Smile!" I said to them.

They looked confused.

I pointed to my mouth. "Smile for the camera!"

Nothing.

So I snapped a few photos of a family who appeared to hold a very cynical view of the world and gave the camera back.

They all bowed and thanked me sincerely in broken English. One man said, "Best of luck."

His words stuck with me. That's not something you just go around saying in a foreign country.

"Thank you," I said.

We crawled into my uncle's vehicle again and drove up to the summit until we were all afflicted with altitude headaches and confusion. The sickness went from moderate to debilitating in a matter of minutes. I couldn't catch my breath. My head felt like it had been clamped in a bench vise.

When we reached the peak, I carried my sister on my hip, my cousin walked beside me, and my uncle led the charge, carrying the cardboard box in his arms.

The view was endless. The sky was so deep it looked infinite. The world below looked small. When we reached the guardrail of an overlook, my uncle squatted and touched my shoulder. He squeezed it and pressed his forehead to mine.

"You're the man," he said. "You're the one who does the scattering, okay?"

"I do the what?" I said.

His voice was quiet, almost lost in the thin air. He smelled like peanut butter. "This is your responsibility now. You have to take care of your mother and your sister. No matter what. That's why you're the one doing the scattering."

The weight of this responsibility scared me. It felt heavy on my shoulders.

"Now, I know it ain't fair," he went on. "But life ain't fair. That's the way life goes. Nothing is fair. You just adjust to it and keep going."

He handed me the box of my father's remains. "You're gonna be alright," he said.

It was a nod of confidence that I did not deserve. I was not a man. In fact, I'd never felt so alone.

I hoped something wonderful would happen on that mountain to make me believe in something bigger than myself. Then maybe I wouldn't feel so alone. Nothing is more dreadful than loneliness.

So I asked the sky for a fairytale sendoff. Maybe then I could quit feeling so angry with him. Maybe if nature erupted in an overture of beauty and hymns, I would forgive him for what he did to us. Maybe if his ashes were greeted by a chorus of clouds, wind, snow, and angels singing, I could rest, knowing that I was not by myself in this universe. That something was watching out for me.

I wanted this more than I had ever wanted anything in my life. I asked heaven for it beneath my breath. I wanted a sign.

My uncle carried a two-foot-long bowie knife, housed in a leather sheath. It was an "Arkansas Toothpick," he told me. It was more sword than knife. It had a brass handle and a wide blade that looked like it was meant for dismembering North Atlantic whales. Ceremony was everything to him.

On our short walk, I became sick. I paused to vomit behind a boulder. I hit my knees and heaved. The box fell to the ground and tumbled down a small slope. I retched until I had nothing left. I wasn't sure if it was from altitude or grief. The two didn't feel very different.

I should've been happy about this day since I was growing

to hate the man in the box. We were saying good riddance to him. This should be a joyous occasion, for we were moving on with our lives. But I wasn't happy about anything. I was just confused.

Since he'd died, I had not been able to pick one emotion and feel it entirely. Why did I hate such a beautiful human being? And why did I love such a wicked man? I was two people trapped in one body.

I looked at the cardboard box, lying on its side. I was too dizzy to cry. My uncle helped me to my feet. He brushed me off. My head throbbed. Pressure built up behind my eyes.

"You're alright," my uncle said. "You're gonna be fine." He held me against himself until I was ready.

We hiked to a rocky spot that caught the midday sunlight in a way that can only be described as art. I could see the edge of the earth, and even farther. The distant towering peaks looked violet and faded. The waves of grain were indeed amber.

Nobody in my family made a sound. My mother did not cry. She was a shell of a woman. My sister was too young to understand, and my cousin was not even in kindergarten. My uncle wore the hard face of a lieutenant sending men into battle.

So it was up to me. I cried for my father. I alone shed saltwater for his memory, even though I hated him. I forced myself to do it because everyone deserves someone to cry for them, even men who try to ruin their own families with guns.

I felt foolish, of course, to be the only one carrying on while my family stood unsmiling. My crying gave way to harder crying, then bawling, with sounds that were almost animal. I lost all control.

My uncle and mother let me finish, their heads bowed. I heard my uncle say to my mother, "He'll be alright."

I finished crying. And my uncle came to me. He draped an arm around my shoulder and said in a whisper, "Look over that direction. See that? That's Oklahoma." He pointed his knife another direction. "I'll bet if you squint hard, you can see Little Rock, where I was born."

I tried to slow my breathing and catch my breath. Crying at high altitude feels a lot like being buried alive in snot.

"See over there?" my uncle said. "That's Texas, probably Amarillo. And that's New Mexico."

We spent a few minutes surveying the scenery. My uncle was trying to give me plenty of time to gather myself.

Finally he said, "You ready?"

I gripped the cardboard box and asked God to help me. In a silent voice, I pleaded for heaven to send something to make me understand. A miracle or something in the sky. I would've been satisfied with a cloud or a few snowflakes. Anything.

My uncle used the knife to slice open the box. Beneath the cardboard was a bag of tan dust compacted in a rectangle. My world went silent. I was holding Daddy. His whole body and mind were in my hands. His dreams, his nightmares, his hopes, his great loves, his very life.

And don't ask me why, but in that moment, I remembered something ridiculous.

I remembered my father, seated at a campfire during a Little League camping trip. There were boys in baseball caps sitting on logs, roasting marshmallows over flames. Their fathers sipped Budweisers and chuckled among themselves.

My father was beside me, two cans deep and in good spirits.

My friend Gary had scented markers in his backpack. I don't know why he had markers on a camping trip, but Gary always was a little weird. My father asked to see the markers.

My father, you see, was a man who liked practical jokes. He loved pranks of all kinds: exploding cigars, leaky fountain pens, hand buzzers, squirting flowers, you name it. He was irreverent, wild, and sometimes downright nuts. With one beer, he could be funny. With two, he was Jerry Lewis.

Gary handed my father a blue marker. It was scented like blueberries. My father removed the cap, sniffed it, and then to everyone's delight, he licked it like an ice cream cone.

The boys howled. Their fathers laughed so hard they nearly passed out.

Next, Daddy bit off the felt tip of a marker like it was a stick of beef jerky. He chewed it, then washed it down with a swig of beer.

"Not bad," he proclaimed. "But needs salt."

The boys and men nearly saturated their jeans.

Next, my father stuck his tongue out. It was stained red and blue. He showed it to everyone. And I loved him for it. He was a performer. A funny man. I was proud to be his that night.

His ashes were so heavy I could hardly hold them. I walked to the railing, overlooking five states and the rest of the known Western world.

And I kept asking the sky for something wonderful to happen. To tell you the truth, I expected it. I really did. I thought I would see wind to kick up a cloud and carry Daddy away in a stunning display of poetry. But life isn't like the movies. No matter how hard you pray, hope, and beg, you can't make your wishes happen. That's not the way life works.

There was nary a cloud in the sky that day. Only sun.

I turned the bag upside down. The humidity had gotten to the ashes. And when I emptied the bag, Daddy fell like a brick, tumbling down the hillside, shattering like a potted plant.

My mother covered her mouth.

My uncle began reciting: "The Lord is my shepherd. I shall not want. He maketh me to lie in green pastures. He leadeth me beside the still waters . . ."

I waited, looking toward the sun. I was waiting for the

company of the heavenly host, for clouds or snowflakes. For God. But nothing happened.

There were no signs, no marvels of the supernatural, no snow, no wind. Not even a bird overhead. My uncle had not finished reciting when I began to walk away.

"Hey," my mother said. "Come back here. Your uncle hasn't even said the Lord's Prayer yet."

"I don't care," I said.

I threw Daddy's empty box into a garbage basket and crawled into the backseat. I felt a change within me. My insides hardened.

It would be a cold day in hell before I said another prayer.

CHAPTER 7

PAPER ROUTES

 We left Georgia and moved to the shores of the Florida Panhandle, not far from the Alabama line. My mother had grown restless in Georgia and could not seem to let roots grow downward. We became gypsies without a wagon, heading for who knows where. But when we hit the sandy soil of Walton County, my mother declared that we were home.

When we first drove across the Highway 331 bridge, which ran from Freeport into the Point Washington State Forest, the sight of the big water made my mother exhale. She had to pull the car over just to admire it. We leapt out and overlooked the water with a sort of reverence.

"Wow," said my sister.

Which was about all anyone could say.

It was on that day that we saw a small boat nearby, trolling the shoreline. A man stood on the bow, working a rod back and forth, operating a trolling motor. My mother waved at him. He waved back. Then we saw the tip of the man's rod bend. We heard his reel zip.

The man removed a beast from the water that was the size of Arnold Schwarzenegger. The great fish had a large black spot near its streamlined tail and reddish color on its back. It writhed in the sun. When the light hit its scales, it sparkled, and I knew what I wanted to do with the rest of my life.

"Hey!" my mother shouted to the man. "What kinda fish is that?"

I almost died. The last thing any self-respecting boy wants is for his mommy to ask ridiculous questions like *What kind of fish is that?* Or worse, *How do you catch one of those?*

"It's a redfish!" the man shouted.

"Wow!" my mother yelled. "How do you catch one of those?"

Oh my God.

"A spoon lure!" the man yelled. Then he held the shiny lure upward so we could see it.

Summers came and went, and I grew up drawing my name on that bay water with cheap outboard motors and a host of spoon lures. I lost bucketfuls of 8/0 hooks, and got even more sunburns. But I took good care of my bay, feeding it every evening with live shrimp and pinfish bait.

Our bank account had become red, and our lives had become unsure. My mother took jobs of all sorts. She cleaned apartments, took care of the elderly, waited tables, and threw the newspaper.

I remember the morning we sat inside my mother's Nissan, running the heat, waiting for the newspaper delivery truck to arrive. I looked at the dashboard clock: 4:29 a.m.

"He's supposed to be here," my mother said, glancing at her watch.

The winter fog was moving across the bay, spilling onto the highway so that you could not see the road. My mother's Nissan was idling before a strip mall. She was sipping coffee from a foam cup, listening to the radio.

"Where in the world could he be?" she said.

There were dark circles beneath her eyes. We were tired and quiet, and the radio was blaring reruns of the Grand Ole Opry like it did every morning. I loved the Opry. I had been playing guitar in earnest ever since my father had died, locked in my room for hours. Music had become very important to me.

Then headlights behind us. The sound of a diesel engine, loud enough to rattle your brain.

My mother turned down the radio. The three of us stepped out of the car before a truck, rubbing sleep from our eyes.

The delivery man wore a thick coat, fingerless gloves, and chewed a cigar. He handed my mother a clipboard.

"Sign here, ma'am," he said.

My mother scribbled on the clipboard and gave it back.

He glanced at the paper and then looked at the raggedy family before him, cold and tired. A smile ran across his face, but not the happy kind. It was a smile of pity.

"Merry Christmas," he said.

"Merry Christmas," we mumbled.

"Happy New Year," my sister said.

He tapped the clipboard. "Five hundred and nine papers," he said. "Yours is the biggest route, you know that?"

"Lucky me," said my mother.

The man deposited a pallet of newspapers as big as a Chevy onto the pavement. He gave my sister and me a few candy canes and a handful of chocolate coins. When he drove away, we stood before the large paper monolith in disbelief.

"That's a lot of newspapers," my sister said.

"What're we supposed to do with those?" I said.

"We wrap 'em," said my mother. "Then we throw 'em. All five hundred and nine."

"That's gonna take all day," I said.

"Yes," she said. "I think it will."

We sat in her Nissan, heater blaring, wrapping newspapers until our hands were black with ink. The sound of the Opry played over the car speakers. It was a rerun broadcast. Don

Williams was singing his anthem about "Amanda." Minnie Pearl was telling jokes, and we were laughing. Never before had I been so grateful to have the entertainment of radio.

When we finished wrapping papers, my mother fired up the engine and said to me, "Call out the addresses, Sean, and hold on."

I read through the list, and she drove in speeding zig-zag patterns all morning, through subdivisions, neighborhoods, and trailer parks. My sister and I were throwers.

Mama would squeal through quiet subdivisions like she was auditioning for the Talladega 500. At each house, my mother would tap the brakes just long enough to induce nausea, and I would throw toward the mailboxes.

"Dadgumit, Sean!" my mother hollered. "Put some shoulder into it!"

At the next house, I threw the paper as hard as I could. The thing turned through the air like a boomerang and hit a large picture window. Glass shattered and made a sound like cymbals crashing.

My mother's eyes became as big as tractor tires. And she did what any God-fearing Deepwater Baptist in her position would've done. She kept driving.

Over time, we became good at our route. In fact, we were a well-oiled newspaper chucking machine. My mother could do the job with her eyes closed, turning circles in neighborhoods one-handed, addresses memorized. She'd ride through trailer parks, apartment complexes, upscale neighborhoods, and gated communities, steering with her elbows, rolling papers at the same time, eating a Moon Pie, and filing her taxes.

There was a kind of urgency in the newspaper business. It was important to deliver the news on time. My mother treated her job like a spiritual discipline. This is probably where I first learned to revere the written word.

One morning, after our route was finished, my mother pulled into the Winn-Dixie, she sipped coffee, and I ate glazed supermarket donuts. She read the paper, and I read the comics section. I heard her sniffing in the seat next to me. She lowered the paper and wiped her eyes. Whatever she had been reading had made her cry. She pointed to the column in the entertainment section.

"A man wrote this column," she said, "and it's really moving." She pinched the bridge of her nose. "You know, you could've written this."

I'm almost certain I blushed. My mother has always had too much faith in me.

"Me?" I said.

"Yes, you. I've read your stories. I know you like to write."

Most of my stories were about things of boyhood interest. A lot of cowboys, and even more shameless women.

I have always enjoyed two things in life. Music and writing. My mother used to tell her friends that if she locked me in a room with a guitar and a typewriter, I would be happy to stay inside singing and writing until the day of my funeral. That's not true. I would have wanted to come out to go fishing now and then.

"Aw, Mama," I said. "Don't be silly. I can't write good."

"Well," she said. "You can't write *well*. I mean . . . you *can* write good."

"You mean *well?*"

"Right. What I mean is, one day *you're* gonna do this—you're gonna write like this. I just know it. Wouldn't you like that?"

She dried her eyes with her sleeve. I didn't know what to say at such a pie-in-the-sky idea. There was no way on earth a flunky like me would ever become a writer.

"And when you do," she said, "I want you to tell them about us. Tell them our story. Will you promise me that?"

I promised.

My mother became my new hero, since the old one had died. She worked different jobs and wore many hats. She cleaned condos, houses, apartments. She worked for a catering company. She was a Chick-fil-A cashier. She had been a member of the workforce since age twelve, serving tables at her uncle's diner. She always labored with a brand of cheerfulness that perplexed me. My mother could work menial jobs with the most devout attitude and make it seem like a privilege worth smiling about. She could make everyone around her smile too. This was her gift.

And on those mornings, throwing papers, we were not miserable, even though we had every reason to be. Those mornings were filled with laughter. Sometimes we would laugh until we cried. Other times, we would cry until we laughed.

Everything good I am comes from my mother. This is why her children joined the workforce early in life. We wanted to be like her. Still do. And over the years, we learned how to imitate her.

When I turned fourteen, I got my first job hanging drywall. I hated it, but it would be the beginning of a long list of manual labor jobs. While my friends were at Choctawhatchee High School, I learned how to read a tape measure.

My schooling isn't a topic I like to discuss. It embarrasses me. But if you've read this far, you deserve to know about it. I went to school only a few times after my father's death. I showed up carrying textbooks beneath my arm and a sack lunch. Students gawked. Teachers seemed unsure of what to say. People scooted away from me in the cafeteria.

I sniffed my armpits for signs of odor. But it wasn't the odor—at least not entirely. I learned that when people don't know what to say, they simply don't do anything.

So I quit school. I'm not proud of it. And I certainly never thought I'd write about it in a book. After all, who wants to read a book written by a guy who quit the seventh grade?

Over time, I became accepted in a world of laborers and dropouts. Construction workers became my friends. Nobody on jobsites cares about your education. Most of my friends did not attend school either.

My buddy Chris, for instance, never made it to the fifth grade. He quit the fourth grade after his father started making better grades in class than he did. And my friend Todd repeated the sixth grade five times and finally got kicked out for trimming his beard whiskers in class. To people of my sort, a strong set of lumbar muscles is more important than learning to diagram sentences.

Sometimes I still wonder how it all happened, and why. We had left Kansas in the middle of a school year, and education had become unimportant. By the time we hit Georgia, my mother could barely find the gumption to keep waking up, let alone enroll me in school. Over time, we found a new routine that didn't include it.

Anyway, I've done more than just construction work in my time. I've worked retail, did landscaping, and once had a short stint as a pizza delivery boy.

I've spent a lot of time working as a dishwasher and a busboy. My mother would drop me off at four in the afternoon at a restaurant in town to do whatever needed doing. The place was a dinner joint. The kitchen smelled weird, the carpet was sticky, and there were stacks of dishes that looked like they'd been involved in a spaghetti homicide.

One night, as I was scrubbing dishes, the general manager of the restaurant came running through the kitchen, hollering.

"Where'd Charlie go?" he yelled. "Where's Charlie? Has anyone seen Charlie?"

Charlie was one of our waiters.

"Charlie called in sick," said one of the waitresses. "So did Sandra. Everybody's got the flu."

The manager freaked. "We're screwed! It's Mardi Gras weekend, and I'm missing two servers! They're gonna mount my head over the fireplace."

Then the manager locked eyes with me. He looked like he wanted to eat me. He said, "You."

"Me?" I said. At the time, I was engaged in a heated battle with a stubborn piece of melted cheese that had been baked onto a tin pan with a blowtorch.

"Yes, *you*, Shane."

"My name's Sean, sir."

"You ever waited tables?"

"No sir."

"Do you want to?"

Are you kidding? Does a bear wash dishes in the woods? Shane Dietrich would rather do anything than scrub a dish.

"Yessir," I said. "I'll do it."

He made me an honorary server. He dressed me in a white tuxedo shirt that was two sizes too big and wrapped a bowtie around my neck. I looked like the Hindenburg zeppelin with freckles.

I pretended to be an adult that night. I used the deepest voice I could muster, and I never let anyone's sweet tea fall below the rim of their glass.

It was a nice change of pace. Serving food is more fun than scrubbing dishes in the back. And it's *a lot* more fun than using radial saws to cut stud pine. It's hard to be in a bad mood carrying dinner above your head. Even better, when you arrive at people's tables, carrying their food, they always seem glad to see you.

It was on that same night, a woman in a black dress came into the restaurant. I'll never forget her. She wore pearls and a green shawl. She sat alone, and she looked at her hands all night.

She ordered a bottle of wine and drank it alone. She never even touched her eggplant parmesan. There was something about her. Something sad. I can spot sadness in a person from ten miles away.

She didn't look like the kind who could handle her alcohol. She looked like the kind who organized carpools and arranged flowers on Sunday mornings.

I handed her a dessert menu. "We have great bananas foster."

She touched the rim of her glass. "No bananas. I want more of this."

I didn't want to give it to her; I knew she had already had enough. Besides, the manager had already taken the liberty of calling her a cab.

"I think you've been cut off," I told her.

So I sat at the table beside her, and I talked to her. I tried to entertain the woman. All I wanted was to see her smile. I told jokes—I have always had a knack for jokes.

It was one of my rare talents. I might not have been able to speak with authority about the Pythagorean Theorem, nor could I name more than three elements of the periodic table, but I could tell you all about the priest and the farmer's daughter.

She didn't want me to leave. So I didn't. I removed my apron and used all my best material until her cab arrived.

By the time the waitresses were mopping floors, and the cooks were scraping the flat-top grills with wire brushes, I had her in stitches.

"Shane!" the manager called to me. "You got dishes piling up."

I glanced into the kitchen and saw a stack of dishes in the sink that was taller than the Chrysler Building. "I'd better go," I said.

The woman paid her bill, stood onto shaky legs, and fell face first onto the floor. I helped her stand upright. She giggled. Then her laughing turned into tears. It was the most forlorn face I'd ever seen—except for my mother's.

"What'll I do without him?" she said. "He was my world."

She placed her head on my shoulder. She sobbed so hard I could feel her muscles tense. I wished I could've said something that would've made her smile, I wished I could've taken hurt from her, but the truth was, I was just as helpless.

"My son found his body," she said. "I hate that man! I hate him! I don't have a dime to my name, what will I do?"

Her husband had hung himself on her son's basketball goal in the backyard, she told me. It sent cold shivers through my body.

When her cab came, I helped her into the backseat of the taxi. And after I buckled her in, she touched my face and said, "You're so young, you've been so nice to me, sorry I ruined everything."

"You didn't ruin anything," I said.

And in that moment, I was overcome with a feeling. I'd told enough jokes for one evening. Now it was time to say something else.

The feeling was one I had never had before. It is the feeling you get when you lie in the surf and relax your body. The waves lift you, then drop you, and something works beneath you that you can't explain. And it is as though all your experiences, the hell you've gone through, the minor triumphs, the pain, the self-doubt, they have been leading to this seemingly irrelevant moment.

But this moment is not meaningless. It's everything. You sense this, right when it's happening. The veil is pulled back, and this morsel of time is perhaps one of the most important moments in your life. It is when you realize that your sole purpose is not just to survive but to help others survive.

I kissed her forehead. I hugged her like she was family. And

I said words I once heard a blind man say: "You're gonna be alright."

She let her weary eyes focus on me. "How do you know?"

"Because I'm proof."

My voice hadn't even dropped yet, and I knew nothing about life. But I believed what I told that woman with all my heart.

Her cab drove away into the night. I was left in an empty parking lot with nothing but my thoughts and the stars above me. It was Mardi Gras. The servers and the cooks were jumping into vehicles, leaving for local parties. One of the waitresses placed several strands of colored beads over my head and said, "You better get home, boy. Your mama's gonna be worried about you."

The lights of our town were all dimming for the night. And I wondered if what I'd told that lady had been true or not. I wondered if my family would be "all right."

I walked the sidewalks home, and I crawled into bed. I slept for a few hours until the alarm started squealing on my mother's nightstand in the other room.

My three-person family shared coffee at 3:45 in the morning. My mother got dressed in sweatpants and boots, my sister wore her pajamas, and we crawled into a Nissan and delivered five hundred and nine newspapers to Northwest Florida.

CHAPTER 8

BAD DREAMS

I woke from a dream. It was a nightmare that didn't end when you opened your eyes. My heart was working double time. I could see things moving in the dark bedroom. Remnants from the memories my father left with us. Something in the corner was coming toward me, moving slowly. I shut my eyes, but I still saw it.

I started shaking. I could barely control my own limbs. My body was cold. I was scared all over.

I wish I didn't have to write this part of the book, but my story makes no sense without it.

The doctors called them night terrors. They were the lingering effects from what happened only twelve hours before my father ended his life. My mother took me to a psychologist who told me I would re-see a lot of things regarding my father, things I tried not to think about when I was awake.

The doc said that the memories would come to the surface at night because my brain would be asleep and unable to suppress them. Not a night went by that these memories didn't come out to play.

The doctor also told me to make sure I drank plenty of water before bed because this would help lessen their severity. Well, no matter how much water I guzzled, I had bad dreams. Some were worse than others.

Usually, I saw a man with a gun. That's one of my greatest hits. It was always my father holding the gun. Sure, I knew he wasn't real. He was only a lingering fragment, but I could see him. I could smell his aftershave. And your body doesn't know the difference between real and formerly real during the midnight hours.

The thoughts were always the same: "Here is a man who is supposed to love me. He is supposed to love us."

But in these dreams, he was trying to kill us.

I sat up straight and whispered. "Don't. Please don't."

But the specter wasn't interested in what I had to say. Bad dreams don't care about your feelings. They are indifferent to you.

That night, I was on the floor beside my sister's bed. I always slept on the floor of my sister's room, ever since my father died. Not in a bed. She had been too afraid to sleep by herself after his death. So I remained on the floor beside her.

Her hand dangled from a mattress above me. She was snoring. I could see the moon through her bedroom window, hear the sound of wind outside. The alarm clock on the nightstand glowed red in the corner.

"You're gonna be alright," I whispered to myself. "Everything's okay."

But I wasn't so sure. I hate to admit it, but I was a boy filled with fear just like everyone else in my family. I was supposed to be the man of the family now. But ever since my father had died, I was scared of everything.

I kicked the blanket off, crawled out of my pallet, and wandered downstairs. My heart was pounding. I sat on the sofa in the dark and turned on the television, keeping it at a low volume.

The low hum of the voices on TV cut my anxiety a little. Sounds of canned laughter were welcome noises.

It was 3:00 a.m., so nothing good was on. I scrolled past sitcoms, talk shows, and infomercials that advertised rotisseries for four easy payments of $39.99. I saw a man selling a speed reading course, claiming a person who watched his videos could read *Gone with the Wind* in forty minutes or less. I watched a half-deranged man advertise OxiClean.

I stopped scrolling when I saw a televangelist. I've always been entertained by televangelists, especially ones with gravity-defying hair. I come from church people who respect the height of hair. But televangelists take this to another level.

This guy was the quintessential holy roller. He had the hairdo and the gold jewelry to go with it. He was shouting so loud that a vein was poking out of his neck. I turned the volume up slightly and tried to forget about bad dreams.

He was begging for money, which was no surprise. Televangelists always ask for money; that was nothing new. At least they did it with more finesse than politicians. The truth is, I owe my very existence to a televangelist—sort of.

Long ago, doctors told my mother she'd never have kids. And she believed them for the first decade of marriage. Until one day, a televangelist pointed to the camera and hollered, "Someone out there wants to have a baby! Believe, and ye shall have a child!" Then that evangelist asked everyone within the television viewing radius to send him their paychecks, Social Security checks, and insulin money. He was going to build a waterpark for Jesus, complete with a tornado slide.

My mother flipped off the television, and she believed this man's words. And if ye can believe it, I was conceived that month.

The sound of the TV was interrupted by a crash on the front porch. I muted the television. In one millisecond, my fears multiplied by ten thousand. This was no dream. This was an actual *noise*.

I heard something moving on the porch. My heart started racing again. I started to tremble so bad that even my teeth were rattling. I hated this about myself, the way fear swallowed me, the way I lost all control of my faculties and believed the worst about the world.

I crept toward the door with a Louisville Slugger resting on my shoulder. It was the same bat I won the Little League regional championships with. My knees were spaghetti. My bat was quivering. I flipped the porch light and threw open the door. I saw a raccoon tail scurrying away.

I wanted to laugh, but I was too emotional.

The televangelist was still on the screen, waving a Bible in the air. He loosened his tie and removed his jacket. He spun in circles, screaming at the camera. I've never been so grateful to see a televangelist before.

I turned up the volume. I suppose I was hoping the man with the funny hair would give me something to laugh about. But that's not what happened.

"GOD SEES YOU!" the holy roller yelled. "AND HE KNOWS THE FEAR YOU CARRY!"

I muted the television.

The man's red face stared straight at me through the screen. He was waving his finger around like televangelists have been doing since the invention of Rolex watches.

Unmute.

"GOD KNOWS HOW TERRIFIED YOU ARE, BUT YE HAVE NOTHING TO BE AFRAID OF, GOD IS WITH THEE . . ."

I muted it again.

"No way," I whispered. "It can't be."

How could this man on TV be saying these exact words at

this exact moment? This guy was a walnut with one liter of Just for Men hair dye in his hair.

Unmute.

"DO NOT BE AFRAID OF THE TERROR BY NIGHT, FOR 'THOU ART MINE' THE LORD HATH SAID!"

Thou muted it again.

This was bizarre. This man in the silk suit looked like he'd fallen off a one-way bus to Branson, Missouri. But there was no denying it, he was talking straight to thou.

A telephone number flashed on the bottom of the screen. I don't know what came over me, but I picked up the phone and dialed it.

I was greeted with inspirational music on the line, played by Dino. I recognized the song right away because my mother loved Dino and often played his records to serenade her while she did household chores like frying chicken, dusting ceiling fans, weeding the driveway, or tarring the roof. The song was "Majesty." I was humming it in a soft voice because I knew the lyrics.

I was raised during a time when Southern Baptists listened to the music of Dino, Second Chapter of Acts, Amy Grant, John Michael Talbot, and the immortal Sandi Patty.

To my mother, Sandi Patty deserved her own book in the Bible. Many women in our church felt the same way. In fact, females in our congregation wanted to *be* Sandi Patty so badly that when *More Than Wonderful* hit Christian bookstore shelves, every woman below age thirty showed up the following Sunday wearing Aqua Net bangs and ruffled secretary blouses.

The music on the phone ended. A woman's voice answered.

"Thank you for calling New Work Zion Hill Foundation of Love and Faith and Healing and Worldwide Mercy Full Gospel Ministries International Incorporated, how much can I put you down for, please?"

I felt ridiculous. I almost hung up. But something in me wouldn't.

"Hello?" the female voice said. "Hello, is someone there? Hello?"

"I'm here," I said.

"Good evening, sir. How much can I put you down for?"

"This was a mistake. I'm sorry I called."

"Wait. Hold up. God don't make mistakes, sir. Maybe I can help you."

I laughed. "*God* didn't make the mistake of calling you, lady. I did. And I doubt you can help me. Have a nice day."

"Oh yeah? Well, *something* made you call. Why don't you try me?"

This lady had already gotten on my nerves. What right did she have keeping me on the line, asking for my money?

"It was that nut on TV," I said. "When he started talking . . . I don't know—it was like he was talking to me."

"It wasn't him, sir. It was the *Good Lowered*."

Right. And maybe the *Good Lowered* wanted to build a waterpark for the starving children in Orlando.

"I don't know what I was thinking," I said. "I shouldn't have called. Sorry to waste your time . . ."

"No! Don't hang up!"

What was wrong with this woman?

"Please," she went on. "We don't get many calls at this hour. I'm here all by myself, and I'm bored. Why don't you talk to me?"

"I don't have anything to talk about."

"You can talk about whatever you want. Start with what Apostle Shambachatayalla said that made you want to call."

"I don't know, ma'am. This is just . . ."

"My name's not *ma'am*. It's Vanessa."

This was getting too personal. I come from a private family.

We did not discuss personal feelings with strangers—or even close friends for that matter. We were private people who, upon entering a bathroom, ran the sink faucet before we did our business.

I said, "I called because I was . . . scared."

There. I admitted it. It felt freeing, a little, just to say it.

"What are you afraid of?"

"It was a dream."

"What was it about?"

I took a giant breath. I didn't *want* to talk about this. In fact, the last thing I want to do right now is keep writing, but I owe it to you.

"The dream was about my father," I said.

"Tell me," she said.

And on that night, something in me *needed* to talk. It was like a festering sore that needed to be drained. So I told this stranger everything. I started from the beginning, and I told her things I'd never told anyone.

I told her about the night my father came home from work and about the argument that erupted. About the disagreement between him and my mother that turned into a war. And about how my mother was losing the battle.

I told her how he lost his mind and began shouting so loud the roof almost detached. How the light in his eyes shifted, and he became another man entirely. I told her how I snuck out of bed only to find him swinging his fists at my mother, screaming. Spit flew from his mouth. He threw my mother around like a rag doll. And even though we tried to stop him, he was empowered with the strength of a maniac.

I told this strange woman how on that fateful night I was so scared I couldn't stop shaking. How my stomach hurt. How I wet myself. How I couldn't swallow, couldn't breathe. How I saw my father remove a handgun from his belt and jam it against my mother's neck. How she pleaded for mercy. How he wouldn't even hear her.

I stopped talking. I was starting to shake so bad the phone almost dropped.

"Bless him, dear *Lowered*," said the woman. "Bless him." And she prayed in what sounded like Italian.

I don't know why I trusted this stranger, but I did.

"Maybe you don't wanna hear this," I said into the phone receiver. "Maybe I shouldn't be telling you this."

"Give him strength, *Jeez's*," she whispered.

I told her how my father had smacked my mother with the butt of the revolver and broke her nose. Then he pushed her backward and beat her like he would've beaten a grown man. He was not the man I knew. He was someone else, invading the body of the man who raised me.

That night, my sister stood beside me and howled.

"What should we do, Sean? What do we do?"

I didn't know what to do. I couldn't answer. What does a good boy do in a time like this? What *should* a boy do?

So I did nothing.

This man, this stranger who had taken my father's body, this terrible man—I didn't know who he was. He was not my baseball-playing, joke-telling, stick-welding, dove-hunting, mountain-loving, ironworking Daddy. This man manhandled my mother into his truck and told her he was going to kill her and then kill himself.

And all I could do was stand idly by, unable to move.

Of course, I knew I had to do something. I couldn't remain motionless while my mother was taken to her grave at the hands of a killer. So I lumbered into action.

My sister wept beside me. I pushed her away. Our dogs were barking at my father. I shoved them from the window. I headed straight for the garage.

The night was so turbulent that the atmosphere had a dull buzz to it, like an unseen fifty-amp electrical panel about to explode.

I paused my story.

"Bless him, *Lowered*," came the voice on the phone. "Bless him, *hallelujah*."

I saw my father drop his gun during their struggle. It slipped out of his hands while my mother flailed against him. It fell in the tall grass. He shoved her in the truck cab and told her to stay put. Then he left my mother to search for the gun in the yard.

That was when my sister shouted, "Do something, Sean! Do something!"

This was my chance. If I was going to do anything, it had to be now. It was now or never. I had to act fast.

My father's shotgun was in its leather case on the top shelf. The same gun we used for shooting dove. The same gun I fired every New Year's Eve ever since I was old enough to spell my name.

I climbed the shelves to retrieve the gun. I loaded it the way he showed me and balanced it against my shoulder. I cried so hard my eyes were blurry.

"Go to the basement!" I shouted to my sister. "I don't want you here."

"Help Mama!" she shouted.

"Go to the basement! Right now! Dammit, go!"

She did not leave. I stood at the window in the garage. The shotgun fore-end was in my grip. I trained the front sight on the man who made me.

"Please," I prayed, holding that gun. "Please help me."

I wanted angels to swoop down and save my mother, my sister, and me. But heaven had turned a deaf ear to us, and we were stuck in the throes of a living nightmare that was only getting worse.

I placed my finger on the trigger. I willed myself to pull it, but my finger wouldn't move. I tried several times to pull, but nothing happened.

Just one finger twitch, that's all it would've taken. My father would've been disabled, and my mother would live to see another sunrise. But it didn't happen that way.

Instead, while my father searched on hands and knees in the dark for his handgun, I put down the shotgun, and I hated myself for it.

My father finally found the pistol, and my heart dropped. I decided I would run toward him and plead with him to spare my mother. I was going to beg the stranger to let her live. But I couldn't make my legs move. He tucked the weapon into his pants and jogged toward the truck. And I knew he would kill her.

But when he reached the vehicle, he found the passenger door open, the dome light glowing, and the cab empty. My mother was gone.

I could see her from where I stood. She was running through a hayfield toward the woods. She ran like I'd never seen her move, high-stepping through the grass like a whitetail, heading for safety.

The crazed man wasted no time. He leapt into his truck, gunned the engine, and drove straight into the field after her. He mowed over the tall grass, headlights blazing. He screamed her name out the window like a lunatic. He bellowed like a man on a battlefield.

But no matter how hard he screamed, he was too late. My mother had escaped.

He was gone for nearly an hour, searching, riding the gravel roads, looking for her along the rural highways. My baby sister and I sat on the porch steps listening for the sound of gunfire, watching for the glow of blue and red lights. My father's search was to no avail. When my father pulled into our driveway, he was empty handed.

He crawled out of his vehicle and hurled his gun into our barn.

It was the strangest thing—my father calm and quiet. I didn't recognize him. There was something odd about him.

He wandered to the garage, laced his shoes, and fuzzed my hair. I could see nothing in his eyes. He was unfamiliar and strange. He spoke with an unusual cadence.

"I've done it this time," he said. "I've really done it."

"What have you done, Daddy?"

And for a glimpse of a second, I saw light flicker in his eyes. The light of the man I once loved.

"We won't be seeing each other for a long while," he said.

"Why, what's gonna happen?" I said.

He didn't answer. He wouldn't answer.

We sat in quiet for what felt like infinity in the musty garage. We were waiting for something, though I wasn't sure what that was.

Finally, I broke the quiet and said, "Why, Daddy? Why?" I was not crying. I was asking for an answer.

But he didn't look at me. Probably because he didn't have an answer.

Soon, blue lights were in our driveway. Our doors and windows were smashed in by men in bulletproof vests wielding rifles. There was a lot of screaming. The dogs barked. My sister hid in the corner behind a chair.

And Daddy. He walked toward the deputies in the blazing flashes of red and blue police lights, fingers laced behind his head. He was tackled to the ground. He was apprehended by the Leavenworth County deputies and placed into the squad car with hands behind his back and steel bracelets on his wrists.

He didn't turn to look at me. The vehicle's tail lights faded into the night. And I never saw my father again.

When I finished my story, I had nearly forgotten anyone was on the other end of the line. I wiped my eyes with my forearm. I was crying so hard I had soaked the phone receiver.

I heard sniffing on the line too. The woman didn't say anything for a few minutes. The television glowed in the living room. The televangelist had long since disappeared, and a man was advertising a pair of steak knives.

"Heavenly Father," Vanessa whispered, interrupting the silence. She was speaking so softly that I almost couldn't hear her. "You know this young man, and you *know* how he feels . . ."

And on that night, a woman in Atlanta, Georgia, prayed for a boy from Walton County, Florida, with more sincerity than I have ever known, before or since.

When we finished, I wandered back to my sister's bedroom and assumed my place on the floor beneath her. She stirred for a moment.

"Sean?" she said. "Are you there?" She reached out a hand, searching for mine.

"I'm right here. There's nothing to be afraid of, Sarah." And I meant it.

I slept like a newborn.

CHAPTER 9

SIX OLD STRINGS

You don't know you're getting older until it's too late. It happens without your permission. You go to bed one night a boy; you wake up the next morning with armpit hair. One Sunday, you discover you can't hit the tenor notes on "Savior Like a Shepherd Lead Me," and your pants are too short.

My friends were becoming interested in girls, but I didn't have much time for them. I was too busy tending to the women already in my life. I had 37 aunts, 109 cousins, a mother, a sister, and 683 neighborhood women who wandered into our house at random just to slap the back of my head and tell me to stand up straight.

Certainly I was *interested* in girls. But girls weren't interested in me. Not even the girls whose lot in life was to take their little brothers to prom. No self-respecting female wanted a suitor who was a dropout, who worked manual labor. Thus many of the girls I approached with ideas of romance suddenly developed incurable diseases or had sudden family emergencies.

Once, I asked a girl on a date, and she answered, "Sorry, I'm getting my cat declawed tonight."

"Oh really?" I said. "I didn't know you had a cat."

"Well, I don't. My older sister has a cat though."

"I didn't know you had an older sister."

"Well, I don't. She's actually my cousin."

"I thought all your cousins lived in Atlanta."

"They do."

"So you're going to Atlanta . . . to get a cat declawed?"

"Well, no, but we're all really worried about the cat."

"Gosh, I'm sorry to hear that. What's the cat's name?"

"I can't remember."

But growing up wasn't all bad. For instance, I had gotten pretty good at playing the guitar and singing. Also, I had armpit hair. Before long, I had even gathered enough money from working construction to buy a truck. I found a beat-up Ford in the paper, paid cash for it, and named it the Jolly Green Giant.

It wasn't a nice truck. The vehicle was missing its front and rear bumpers. The tires were mismatched sizes. Whenever I drove faster than twenty miles per hour, the steering column would vibrate so much that it felt like I was having a grand mal seizure. Still, I don't know if I had ever been any happier than I was the day I parked that vehicle in the driveway.

For some people, the transition into adulthood happens almost overnight. It certainly did with me. I've met other orphans. We are kids who can't even pinpoint when this change happened. We have felt like old people since our fathers died.

Our mothers looked to us for big decisions. They relied on us. Before we ever went out on our first date, we were already acting like a retired father of four. All our paychecks went toward rent. All our spare time went toward helping to keep a home fire burning.

We got so good at pretending we were older than our age that we started to believe it. We begin to hate our own reflections because they betray how we see ourselves. The mirror portrays us too young. We are not children; we are ancient. We're fifty years old thirty-five years before our fiftieth birthday.

Except around members of the opposite sex.

A pretty girl changes everything. She can bring out the youthfulness in a parentified child. No longer is this child so shrewd or responsible. His IQ is reduced to asphalt-level intelligence. That's how it happened with me.

She was pretty. I was sixteen. We couldn't have been more different. Her people were Methodist, and mine didn't even allow cough syrup in the house.

She came from New Orleans. I lived in the sticks of Walton County. She had blond hair, blue eyes. I had red hair, white skin, and birdlike features that prompted strange elderly women to appear out of nowhere and try to feed me.

She drove her daddy's Lexus. I drove a truck with a front bumper made out of a two-by-four, with colored Christmas lights wrapped around it.

On the night I met her, I met her car first.

I drove along the dirt road, winding toward the bay. My one good headlight lit the dirt path ahead of me. I arrived upon a clot of rusty trucks. I pulled alongside a red Lexus that looked like it had just left the showroom.

"You're late," said Chubbs, tapping on my window. "I've been waiting for you for fifteen minutes."

I leapt out of my vehicle. "Whose car is that?" I asked.

He shrugged. "Some chick who just moved to town. Did you bring it?"

I peered into the Lexus windows. It was not the kind of car you expect in North Walton County.

"Leather seats," I said. "And look at that stereo."

"Did you bring it?" he said.

"You gotta show me the money first," I said.

Chubbs reached into his drawers and removed a wad of cash that was soggy with sweat. He held it outward. "Go ahead. Count it."

"Why was that money in your pants?"

"It wasn't in my pants. It was in my underpants. Here, take it."

I swatted him away. "Are you nuts? I'm not touching that money. I could get a yeast infection."

"C'mon, do you really think *my* sweat is any more disgusting than anyone else's?"

"I'm not going to dignify that remark."

I used my handkerchief to take the floppy dollars and almost gagged. I tucked them into my pocket and then gave him an old guitar case in return. He removed a beat-up instrument and held it to the moonlight.

"Wow," he said. "This thing looks old."

"That's because it *is* old."

"You sure you don't mind parting with your old man's guitar?"

"I don't mind."

Chubbs positioned the instrument on his knee. The guitar once belonged to my father. Chubbs strummed a chord. He sang. His voice rang across the night with the gentle sensitivity of Elmer Fudd.

My father bought that guitar when he was a boy. He had always wanted to learn to play, but he never did. So it was passed to me.

It wasn't a nice guitar—it was a glorified piece of junk. My uncle John taught me to play it, and we discovered that I was a natural. In fact, music was one of the only things I could do well.

My father loved to hear me play and sing. It was one of the only things I ever did that made him look at me with proud eyes. His pride was hard to come by.

During childhood I wanted nothing more than to see that proud look on his face. So I learned to sing all his favorite songs, every hymn, traditional tune, honkytonk ballad, and cowboy song. I did it to make him smile.

But when he died, something changed inside me. I didn't want to touch that guitar again. And I didn't care if he was proud of me or not. In fact, I didn't ever want to hear his name again. I didn't even consider myself his boy anymore. Like I said, growing up can change a kid.

Chubbs and I walked to the beach. He brought the instrument along. In the distance, I saw a bonfire roaring, sending sparks upward into the darkness. The bay was smooth and black in the night. The moon was out.

Kids surrounded the fire by the dozens. Teenagers sat on the shore beneath tall pines, engaged in nocturnal rebellion. Some teenagers were smoking cigarettes, sipping from bottles they'd stolen from their parents' cabinets.

"I gotta go," I told Chubbs. "My mama's waiting on me."

"Oh no," he said. "You haven't seen the guitar's maiden voyage. I'm about to christen this thing."

"I can't."

"C'mon, ten minutes, that's all I ask."

I agreed.

I found my way to a log beside the fire, where people were sitting. Behind me was Billy Wilkerson, lying in the sand, singing into the palm of his hand, "The wheels on the bus go round and round . . ."

I sat beside the girl who was by herself. She was pretty, with blond hair.

"Hi," she said.

"Hi," I said.

She didn't seem like the others. It seemed as though she hailed from a better realm than the rest of us peasants. She was sophisticated, tall, and sat with poise. I have always had the same slouching posture as Barney Fife.

There was a white cast on her leg with signatures all on it.

"You must be an actress," I said.

"Huh?" she answered.

"Your leg," I said, pointing to her cast. "You broke a leg."

She gave me a laugh. Then she looked at me. Most girls looked through me or past me. This one saw me. I almost slipped into a coma and forgot my own name.

"Hey!" Chubbs shouted, holding the guitar on his lap. "This thing is almost as old as my dad! It says fifty-eight on the label inside!"

"Congratulations," I said.

Chubbs strummed, using a quarter for a pick. He played a few bars of a tune that sounded like a chainsaw tearing through a ukulele factory.

People laughed at him, but he kept singing.

His voice carried across the water, all the way into the next county. Most of the kids weren't listening. They were talking about things related to high school. They talked about football, track, cheerleading, and teenage life. I felt like a moron around such kids.

These people knew things I didn't. They had ordinary existences, and all the things that came with them. They knew about love notes in class, algebra tests, fussy teachers, how to write essays, proms, and homecoming games. I knew how to clean the filter on a shop vac with the air hose.

I watched my buddy Chubbs sing "Mandy" to a young coed sitting beside him. She wore a terrified look while he thrashed at the strings with the same ferocity you'd use to scrub barnacles from a boat hull.

"You're awfully talkative," the girl beside me said.

"Just naturally gabby, I guess," I said.

"You don't wanna be here, do you?"

"Does it show?"

"So why're you here then?"

Well, I wasn't sure. I suppose, looking back, the real reason I was there was because I couldn't leave that guitar. I had certainly sold it, but I couldn't walk away from it. I was so convinced that I hated my father, but sometimes I wasn't so sure that was the case. I had hoped getting rid of the guitar would feel like ridding myself of him. It didn't.

As soon as Chubbs touched the instrument, it only made memories more vivid. And I wasn't sure if I hated my father or if I hated myself for loving him so much.

I tried to forget that the wood on the guitar neck still bore the oils from my father's hands and that the finish was stained from things my father spilled on the surface during his boyhood.

Finally, Chubbs stopped playing and walked toward me. He extended the guitar to me and said, "Here, play something. My voice is starting to hurt."

"No thanks," I said.

"C'mon," said Chubbs. "I can't keep being awesome all night. I have to rest."

"I'd rather not."

The girl scooted so close to me that her thigh was touching mine. I could smell her shampoo.

"Oh, please," she said. "Play us something."

A boy will do all sorts of things when he smells shampoo.

I stared at the guitar. There was a chunk of wood missing from the edge of the soundhole. That happened when I fell down the stairs as a nine-year-old. I had been playing in the stairwell because the acoustics were good. Miraculously, the guitar survived the fall.

I took the guitar. I tuned it, turning the knobs on the headstock. I felt everyone's eyes on me. I felt her eyes on me. An electric jolt ran through my neck and shoulders. It worked its way into my head and behind my eyes. It was the piercing idea that my father held this same guitar when he was my age.

The redheaded man who used to love me. Who once

paddled a fishing skiff on a small waterway, singing at the top of his voice.

I touched the strings, and I played the first song that came to my mind:

> Will the circle be unbroken
> By and by, Lord, by and by?
> There's a better home awaiting
> In the sky, Lord, in the sky.

I sang until I lost myself in the lyrics. I closed my eyes and forgot all about the teenagers around me. I forgot about the way I felt, and about my lack of confidence. With this guitar in my hands, I was no longer just an uneducated hick—I was me. Whoever that was.

When I got to the third verse, I felt hot streaks of water fall across my cheeks. All of a sudden I quit playing and set the guitar on the sand. The mood of the party died.

Chubbs slapped my back and said in a soft voice, "Don't cry, man. You weren't *that* bad."

The girl placed her hand on mine. Her hand was cold, and there were tears in her eyes too.

"That was beautiful," she said.

I reached into my pocket and gave Chubbs his soggy money back.

CHAPTER 10

AND IT WAS MARY

Her name was Mary. We spent the summer together. We did things that teenage summer romances require. I took her to ride roller coasters in Panama City, I won her a stuffed animal at the horseshoe toss, and I rang a bell with a giant hammer to prove that I was strong. We took boat rides on the bay. We went to movies. I gave her the key to my truck toolbox.

During this time, I had formed a country-western band. Mary never missed a chance to see us play. Even when we played at the hardware store on Saturday mornings to help Mister Alvin sell refurbished lawn mowers on the sidewalk. Mary loved our music, and even though we were god-awful, she was a faithful devotee.

"Maybe this is what love is," I thought. I felt like a *young* man around her, not like the old man of my house. I felt alive.

It only took a few dates for me to realize we weren't exactly made for each other. Even so, we got along. We didn't argue, we were polite to each other, and that counted for a lot. She seemed glad to have me around, and I was happy to not be alone.

She liked the way I talked, and she enjoyed hearing the elaborate jokes I had memorized. She wanted to be a physician one day.

Her family was wealthy. Her father drove a car that cost more than my kidney would fetch on the black market. Her family's living room was big enough to host the Women's British Open. Her mother's pocketbook cost more than it would take to feed a small Haitian village for a month. Her home was four stories tall, directly on the Gulf of Mexico, with granite countertops, vaulted ceilings, and central vac. Central vac.

They had a maid named Belinda, who cooked whatever the family wanted, washed clothes, and mopped floors. Belinda was my favorite member of the family. She was an older black woman with cropped white hair. She said very little to her employers, but she could talk a blue-streak to me. I'm not sure why she felt so warm toward me, except that she went to the Missionary Baptist Church, so we were technically in the same denomination.

"I don't know what you see in Mary," Belinda once told me. "She's a spoiled thing. Don't get me wrong, I love that child, but you gonna get your heart broke."

Of course, I knew she was right. Deep down, I knew Mary was miles above me. But when I held her in my awkward arms, I felt like somebody important. And it was fun to pretend, every now and then, that I wasn't the world's most loveable loser.

Still, sooner or later it dawned on me. Mary wasn't a very kind person sometimes. Once, I overheard Mary tell Belinda she wanted lasagna for supper. So Belinda painstakingly made a lasagna from scratch. Belinda was a magnificent cook. I could write a chapter about her lasagna, but I'm not going to. When the casserole came out of the oven, Mary wouldn't touch it because the tomato sauce was too—and I quote—"yuck-yuck."

"Eeww," said Mary, stabbing her plate like it was about to squirt ink on her. "I can't eat this, Belinda!" And she pushed the plate away.

Belinda simply removed the plate, scraped the lasagna into the garbage, and then made a *brand-new* lasagna that was less yuck-yuck. It took another few hours to prepare. By the time it was done, Mary wasn't hungry anymore. She'd already eaten cereal.

That same night, Belinda sent me home with bucket loads of lasagna. "Sssshh," she said. "Don't tell Mary I done gave it to you." I ate the whole thing between two stop lights on the way home.

My friends couldn't stand Mary. Once, I introduced her to some fellas I worked with at a party. She behaved oddly around them. When she shook the hands of my buddy Dale, I could tell Mary was nauseated by boots and denim.

When Mary left to visit the ladies' room, Dale took me aside and said, "Are you outta your mind? You can't date this girl."

"Why not?" I said.

"Because she probably uses a gold toilet brush."

"Huh?"

"She was born with a silver spoon in her hand."

"You mean her mouth."

"Exactly."

"Are you saying she's too good for me?"

"No, I'm saying *you're* too good for *her*. C'mon, wake up. She's one of *them*."

"Them?"

He slapped my chest. "You idiot. She's from the *other side*."

"The other side of what?"

"Of the tracks, you dork! She's *old money*, a *trust-fund baby*. She's a *saddle-my-horse-Charles* kinda girl."

I started to understand what he was saying. Of course, I'd suspected this all along, but I was too dense to pay attention to it. People from my world believed in two kinds of people: *Us* and *Them*.

If you were *Us*, you wore blue jeans, cotton. If you were *Them*, you did not drink beer from a can.

If you were *Us*, at least once in your life you asked, "What's a *cul-de-sac*?" If you were *Us*, your vehicle had less mileage on it than your home. If you were *Us*, your mothers knew how to feed a family on lard and flour. If you were *Them*, you might have grown up asking things like, "What's lard?"

By the end of the summer, I knew I would never be one of *Them*, no matter how hard I hoped. And one night, over supper, it was time for Mary to cut me loose.

She tried to break the news gently at a Mexican restaurant. The waiter had just brought our cheese dip.

"Things just aren't working," Mary said. "I'm sorry, but it's school and stuff, and it's all got me stressed out."

"School doesn't start for another few weeks."

"Well, I mean, I'm *about* to be stressed out with school, you know?"

"Hey, don't worry about anything. We can handle it."

"No, I don't think we can. What I mean to say is, well, I'm just so confused right now, so confused with where my life is going."

"I get confused sometimes too, but it will pass."

"You don't understand. I'm not confused. I lied about that."

I stopped eating, mid-chip. I could see it laid out before me. I knew what she was trying to say.

"I wanna see other people," she said.

"Other people?"

"Yeah, I wanna live a little, and you should too. You should really do something with your band—you're good. You should be young, you know?"

"I should?"

"Yeah, because you're a *great guy*."

Oh no. Nobody wants to be a *great guy*. Your uncle Herb is a *great guy*. Your friend's step-dad, who sometimes walks around his house naked even though he has company, is a *great guy*.

Then I had this feeling that Mary wasn't being honest.

"There's someone else, isn't there?" I said.

She didn't have to answer.

She'd been going around with a kid named Mark. Mark was a boy who worked at his father's firm in Pensacola. He was tall, dark, handsome, and a track star. He had shoulders that measured fifteen feet across, and his truck had matching tires that belonged on a bulldozer.

He played his radio too loud, wore his hat backwards, drove too fast, and spoke about things like mutual funds just because he could. His hair was long, with a gentle wave to it, and he had dimples.

How could I compete with dimples? I left the Mexican restaurant that night feeling like the biggest waste of God's oxygen. I was angry with myself, with the world. I wanted to run away and make a new life for myself in, say, Winnipeg or Nova Scotia. I blamed myself for not being the kind of guy Mary wanted.

So that night, I drove until I couldn't drive any farther. I drove until the scenery of Northwest Florida gave way to the farmland of Alabama. The world was nothing but a collection of small towns and longleaf pine outside my window. And I was not allowed to be part of this world.

Soon, I was far out into the country, where the only light came from the stars. I parked in a large, scalped field beside a round cotton bale, and I stayed there for hours. I was a fool to ever think I could be anything other than what I was.

My father, the ghost, lingered nearby. I could feel his presence, stoic, like a heron, looking at me.

"What do you want?" I said.

Daddy said nothing.

I wanted to shout something at him, something cruel, something hurtful. But I didn't want to expend the energy. Besides, you can't hurt a dead man's feelings. They don't have any.

After a few days of sulking and wallowing in puddles of self-pity, I decided to try to win Mary back, like they do in romance movies.

It was a horrible idea, but it came to me one evening while my aunts were watching *An Officer and a Gentleman* on TV. "Of course!" I thought to myself. I would do what all Hollywood men did. I would show up on her doorstep with a bouquet and a pressed white shirt and lay my heart open. If I were lucky, everything would work out like it did in every Richard Gere movie ever made.

I appeared on her porch one evening. I sported a white button down and khaki ensemble—courtesy of the Baptist thrift store. And new shoes. Well, at least they were new to me.

I rang the doorbell. I straightened my collar. I heard footsteps. I started to tremble. I felt like a groveling fool. I saw someone peek out the window.

And I finally understood.

I knew I wasn't on that doorstep because of love. I was there because I was afraid of not being loved, and those two things are very different. Fatherless kids will do odd things to avoid being unloved. They will pretend to be people they aren't. They'll lie if need be. They'll squeeze their fat feet into thrift-store shoes, buy bouquets, and spend money they don't have. But you can't make something true just because you want it to be. You can't be someone you aren't, and you can't make people feel things they won't.

So I decided I would give Mary the flowers, wish her well, and bid her goodbye forever. We would hug, go separate ways, and I would not beg. I would resume a life of an uneducated putz who helped pay his mother's rent. I would continue driving my god-awful truck around town, and if ever I saw her in the Winn-Dixie, I would turn and walk the other way.

The door opened.

It was not Mary. It was her mother who appeared. The woman wore a dim face when she saw me.

I extended the flowers. "Good evening, Mrs.—"

But before I could get the words out, she interrupted me. "You need to leave, now."

It felt like a slap to the face with a cinder block.

"Ma'am," I said, "I just came to give these flowers to Mary—"

"She doesn't wanna see you."

"I know, but you don't understand. I'm not trying to—"

"My husband and I don't want you hanging around anymore, do you understand? It's over between you two."

It was like being kicked in the gut by a linebacker.

She tried to close the door, but my feelings were too hurt to let her slam a door in my face. I stepped forward and placed my foot in the doorjamb.

"Please," I said. "Will you just give these to her? That's all I ask."

She stepped out onto the porch and shut the door behind her. "Listen to me, Sean . . ." The way she said my name is something I have never been able to unhear. It was as though it hurt her to say it.

"You're a nice boy," she went on, "but let's be honest, you're going nowhere . . ."

I wanted to disappear forever. Someone drop me into the bay and let a starving bull shark have his way with my internal organs.

"You're not even in high school," she said. "Look at yourself. Where is your future? I'm sorry. I really am. Mary got your hopes up. We tried to tell her to leave you alone. I'm sorry she led you on. Now leave this porch, and don't come back. Good night."

The door shut.

I walked to my truck. The Christmas lights on my bumper

were glowing multicolored in the darkness. Uneducated, poor, stupid, and futureless—I might as well have been a beggar on their porch shaking a tin cup.

When I neared my truck, I saw Belinda, smoking a cigarette, leaning against my tailgate. A cloud of blue exited her mouth. She offered me one. I refused.

"Are those daylilies?" she said, nodding at the bouquet. "I love daylilies."

"Well, today's your lucky day."

She smelled the flowers. She grinned. "Why you got all them Christmas lights on your truck?"

"Because I love Christmas."

"Even in the summer?"

"Especially in the summer."

"Me too."

She sniffed the flowers again and gave me one of her trade-marked smiles. "You ain't gonna cry for that girl, is you?"

"I might."

"Well, you shouldn't. God just saved you from a mistake. That's how God do, save us from mistakes. Hurts like the devil, but the mistake woulda hurt a lot worse."

"I'm not sure God has anything to do with me."

"Oh, he do."

Belinda stomped out her cigarette and placed her hands on my shoulders. "Look at me," she said. "Don't want you crying for that girl, you hear? Not a drop. She don't deserve it, not after what she done."

I nodded.

She shook my shoulders. "You hear me, child?"

"Yes, ma'am."

She patted my cheek. "Good boy. You can bet she ain't gonna be crying for you tonight, so you don't go giving her all your saved-up tears."

"Yes, ma'am."

"You promise me, now."

"I promise, Belinda."

She pulled me into herself. She hugged me hard.

And I broke my promise.

CHAPTER 11

PORTRAIT OF THE BAPTIST
AS A YOUNG MAN

It was a dingy bar. Our band was playing. The audience was listening to our country waltz. My friend Dewey was playing fiddle so sweetly it made my chest sore. Southern Baptists like me were not supposed to be in places like this, but I've always liked living on the edge.

The elderly couple on the dance floor recognized the first few bars of the tune.

"Darlene!" the old man said to his bride. "They're playing our song!"

The two white-hairs swayed along with the music, and if you've never seen two elderly people dance, you need to get right with the Lord.

Our band never sounded so good. I played an old guitar that once belonged to a man I knew, a man I no longer considered my father. He was just a stranger who loaned me his goofy looks and lanky arms. Nevertheless, the guitar felt like it belonged in my hands.

The music ended. People applauded. The elderly couple asked the band to play the same waltz again.

"Again?" said Dewey. "Don't you wanna hear another tune instead?"

"No," said the old man. "That's our song, and it's the only one I care about."

So Dewey began playing the same waltz again, only faster than before. And people danced with the same sincerity. The old couple leaned onto one another and danced like they'd been born on a pinewood floor. The woman in the man's arms reminded me of my mother. A simple woman, with kind eyes.

My mother always said that life moved like a waltz. And I think she's right. It swings back and forth in three-quarter time instead of marching forward in four, like a military advance.

At least, that's how our lives were moving. It felt like we were moving round and round on the same floor, turning circles but never going anywhere.

My mother, God bless her, was dancing with the world on her shoulders, weary but still moving. The music doesn't stop because you're weary.

Waltzes don't move forward. They meander like creek water with an unpredictable destination. The fiddler moves his bow slowly, the guitarist strums on *two* and *three*, the band keeps a lazy but dependable tempo. On the dance floor, the fella in boots leads his lady across the great chasm that divides man and music. It's gentle music. Not at all like four-beat rock and roll.

Waltzing couples can spin in ovals to songs like "Tennessee Waltz," "Home on the Range," or "I'm so Lonesome I Could Cry." They intersect with other dancers, avoiding near collisions, stepping left, then right, then left, then right. Never forward. Her dress catches the air behind her. He smiles. It's the dance of my people. We span the country from the pulp mills of the South to the automotive plants of the North.

And this is our dance. On this floor, working men become artists, and women in cotton dresses become our muses. And when the dancing stops, you find yourself standing in almost the same place you began. You haven't gone anywhere. So you ask the band to play another one.

And so it was with me. My life went nowhere. I turned and spun and kept triple time until one day I was several years older but poorer, still just treading water.

My boyhood had all but disappeared. I was a young man with calloused hands who taught younger men to use electric drills on the jobsite. Men my age had long since graduated high school and gone to college, and now they were starting families of their own and thinking about things like adequate health insurance. But I was still turning in large figure-eights on a dance floor.

My family was a skeleton crew. My mother still worked hard hours. So did my sister. And over time, I forgot all about the quiet little boy whose childhood never was, just like I'd forgotten all about fathers and sadness and baseball and girls.

I tried hard to become a version of myself that didn't even remember Daddy, but it wasn't easy. It takes a lot of effort to forget someone. You can't be yourself while trying to forget at the same time. You start to fill up with contempt, and the contempt smothers you, leaving no space for the real you inside. And you lose yourself. I missed my father, though I wouldn't admit it to myself. No sooner would I miss him than I would hate him again. Then I would miss him. Then hate him. On and on it went. Circles.

In the mornings, I would wake up hating him so bad I wanted to change my name. But by the afternoons, I would be in a supermarket and see a father and son, shopping the produce aisle, and I would become a small child all over again. I would abandon my shopping basket, walk to my truck, and start missing a dead man.

That's enough about that.

When the dancers finished, they clapped again.

"Play another waltz!" said the elderly man, removing his ten-gallon hat, rolling up his sleeves. He was sweating through his shirt.

"Another waltz?" said Dewey. "Aren't you sick of waltzing?"

But the dancers begged. So, we played the "Tennessee Waltz." Everyone loves the "Tennessee Waltz," even people who've never been to Tennessee.

This happens to be the first country waltz I learned to play. I learned it with this band I'm telling you about, a group mostly composed of middle-aged, frustrated cowboys who never learned to rope or ride.

At my first gig, these fellas lied to the manager of a beer joint and said I was eighteen years old. The manager looked at my smooth face and smirked. I'm certain he knew better, but he never said a thing about it. He let me in, and it was the greatest night of my life. On that stage, I was somebody, not a dropout who repulsed the opposite gender.

The day of my actual eighteenth birthday, we were playing in that same beer joint, strumming the same music for the same roomful of people. And I saw that manager again.

He approached me and said, "So today's your eighteenth birthday, huh?"

"Yessir," I said.

He lowered his eyes and said, "I thought you were eighteen a few years ago."

Dewey interceded. He threw his arm around the manager and said, "You know how it is when you're young—time slows down."

The manager smiled. He removed a fifty-dollar bill, tucked it into my shirt pocket, and winked. "Happy eighteenth birthday, Sean."

It is for this reason that establishments like this are forever special to me. People in these worldly joints treated me like family, and in many ways they were the only family I ever knew. They didn't care what my station in life was. In these walls you could be a tile-layer, a sheetrock man, a thoracic surgeon, or a finance attorney. Everyone was the same.

To my friends in the band, I was no longer Sean the Loser. I was Sean the Musician. I played the piano, the guitar, and for traditional Cajun music, the accordion. Their confidence in me made me a better person. Soon, music became the main thrust of my life. I couldn't wait to get off work and meet my friends to play a few waltzes or squeeze the bellows of a twelve-bass accordion on a Cajun melody.

Thus the Southern Baptist boy learned to play music in places lit by neon signs. Although I was uneducated and poor, in this room I was a troubadour, an artist even.

I grew up here. Men in the band taught me how to act like an adult, how to save my money, and how to transpose "Stars of Alabama" into a singable key.

These were my heroes—only, they were not heroes to anyone else. They survived on bad habits, low sleep, and shallow bank accounts. They lived in their cars sometimes, traveled wherever music took them, were not above handouts, and were perpetually in trouble with the women in their lives.

We finished the "Tennessee Waltz," and the people clapped. The elderly couple sat, out of breath.

A man with a white cowboy hat asked us to play "Waltz across Texas."

I looked at the bassist in a panic and said, "I don't know the chords to this song."

He laughed. "Ain't that life, son? Once you finally learn how to play the dang song, it's almost over. I'll help you."

So I learned how to play the waltz during the waltz itself. And maybe that's what my mother meant when she said life was that way.

Maybe the circle keeps moving, and maybe you keep finding new ways to move on the dance floor, even if your moves are all wrong. Eventually, you learn to keep time in your own manner, no matter what happens, just as long as you just don't stop turning.

Friends come and go. Lovers hold you, whisper sweet things, and a few years later they've forgotten your name. Members of your Little League baseball team have shed their baby fat, graduated high school, finished college, and soon they wouldn't even be able to pick you out of a lineup.

Mothers keep throwing newspapers, cleaning condos, manning deep fryers. They keep loving you with all their hearts. No matter which kinds of sinful joints you frequent, you know her Southern Baptist prayer group prays for you.

And early one morning, before the sun is up, you awake to the sound of an alarm. You lie in bed with your eyes open, only to discover that you are in your twenties, and your joints hurt from loading lumber and spending days on your knees with a trowel.

Life is moving at a breakneck tempo. You're not sure if this is good or bad.

You're sleeping on the pull-out sofa in your mother's house. No wonder your lower back is so stiff—the mattress is about as thick as a sheet of single-ply toilet paper.

But you are happy for the first time in your life, and you're finding this feeling through music. The night before, you were up late, playing until the wee hours for people who wanted to hear one waltz after another. You're so tired you can hardly see. It seems like you only shut your eyes a few minutes ago. But you are glad.

You stumble out of the bedroom, wearing your cleanest dirty shirt, and you find your mother cooking breakfast. She has done this every morning since your birth. This little woman, whose husband tried to ruin her, who works hard, who stays cheerful, she's still at it.

She stands over a skillet, flipping eggs in boiling grease, just the way you like them. On a small radio, sitting in the window-sill, there is happy music. She loves music.

You grin when you see her. How does she do it? How can she be so upbeat when life offers little to be so happy about? Maybe it's the music. Maybe music does the same thing for her as it does for you.

This fundamentalist woman sways to the melody, and it blesses your heart. She looks older than you remember. But then, so do you.

You've leaned on each other. Held each other. You have seen her cry enough to fill an aboveground pool. She has watched you do the same. Together you've both thrown enough newsprint to blanket the entire Southeast. This woman didn't just raise you; she grew up with you.

Now her hair is no longer brown and curly. It is gray. And you are full-grown. And the two of you alone are the only ones left who remember John Dietrich. The only two who share the same wounds he left you with. But somehow, though he hurt her more than he ever hurt you, she does not have the same distaste for him that you do. Maybe it's because she's a saint. You've always suspected this.

You sneak up behind her. You hold her close. She is five-foot-two and slight. Her silver hair falls into her eyes. And you dance with her. Right in her own kitchen.

"Hey!" she says with a laugh. "Goodness! Put me down, Sean! Have you lost your mind?"

The spatula is still in her hand, but she's not resisting. She's too happy to be in your arms because you are all her life is about.

You both turn in circles the same way you've seen people do in honky-tonks since you were a teenager, playing with that band you shouldn't have. You twirl her once, twice, three times. Your mother spins as though she were born on a dance floor. Then you kiss the cheek of this beautiful woman with Scottish heritage, a drop of Sioux Indian in her blood, and news-ink-stained hands.

"What on earth has gotten into you this morning?" says the Baptist lady, fixing her hair.

"Mama," I said. "They were playing our song."

CHAPTER 12

CATHEAD BISCUITS

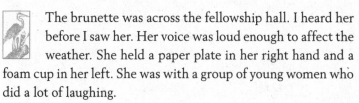

The brunette was across the fellowship hall. I heard her before I saw her. Her voice was loud enough to affect the weather. She held a paper plate in her right hand and a foam cup in her left. She was with a group of young women who did a lot of laughing.

The potluck line stretched from the fellowship hall to the Sunday school classrooms. There must've been fifty people waiting. I was at the tail with my friend, Dewey. Dewey was Catholic, but on Wednesday night potlucks, he was as Deepwater Baptist as George Beverly Shea. The line moved so slow. Dewey and I were about to die from low blood sugar.

"I can practically taste the fried chicken," Dewey said.

I didn't hear him. I was too busy watching the girl with the loud voice on the other side of the room.

When we finally neared the folding tables, Dewey had the shakes. He loaded his plate with so much food his paper plate threatened to collapse.

"You can't take that much food at once," I warned him.

"Why not?" he said.

"Because of *them*."

"Who?"

I shushed him and then pointed to the white-haired women of God who lingered beside the tables, swatting their empty hands with wooden spoons, giving us the stink eye.

"Don't be greedy," one lady said to Dewey. "The Good Lord doesn't like greed."

He hung his head in shame, something most Catholics rarely feel.

A little moral disapproval never hurt anyone.

When I wandered through the line, these women treated me the same way they treated him. These were tough women. They could behead a frying hen without batting an eyelash, drain the blood from the chicken's corpse, and in less time than it took to recite the Pledge of Allegiance they would pluck that bird naked. You do not fool with women like this.

I took two drumsticks with great caution. Then I looked in both directions and took two more.

"You're walking on *very* thin ice, Sean," said one church lady.

I've been a Baptist my whole life. My father converted to fundamentalism when I was a baby. He became evangelical because, as he once said, "It's more fun to drink beer when your friends are teetotalers."

My childhood was lived out in churches. I went through many rites of passage beneath the roof of a house of worship. I learned how to play Texas Hold'em behind the Baptist storage shed. I first learned to play piano in an empty Sunday school classroom. I had my first teenage kiss in the choir loft. I ate my first slice of pound cake at dinner on the grounds. I sang my first song in public with my guitar on a church altar.

These were my people. And even though I found it harder to fit in with them the older I became, they were still mine, and they always will be.

My people weren't exactly fun people. We were the kind who read our Bibles from front to back once per year—or in my case, pretended to. We memorized so many verses that we sometimes used *thee* and *thou* in everyday conversation.

We did not believe in things like secular music, R-rated movies, electrified instruments, *Rolling Stone* magazine, tobacco, *Sports Illustrated*, nylon jogging suits, certain species of penguins, Suzanne Somers, and the like.

Everything was off-limits. Most of the people within our congregation didn't drink, and if they did, they at least had the decency to keep their beer in the garage refrigerator. They did not approve of playing music in taverns, or steel guitars, or Hank Williams. They did not believe in kissing, heavy petting, or pre-marital sex because these things could lead to dancing.

Still, you couldn't have pried me away from this church using a crowbar. I was one of them. Even though I spent evenings playing music for cash, they still let me accompany worship on the old Mason & Hamlin piano for Sunday services, Wednesday night services, and Saturday night prayer meetings. I suppose they believed it would do me some good.

I loved playing music at church. Some of my happiest memories have taken place on Sunday mornings.

When Dewey and I finished fixing our plates, the church ladies investigated our food for signs of gluttony.

"That's an awful lot of squash casserole for just one man," she said to Dewey.

"Yes, ma'am," he said. "I'm sorta hungry today."

"I'd better be able to see my reflection in that plate when you're finished."

"But my plate's made of paper."

"Don't toy with me, you little cuss."

Dewey and I looked for seats in the fellowship hall. I found the table with the loud girl. I sat across from her. The first thing she said to me was, "Would you mind getting me more tea?"

At first, I was confused. I'd never even met this young

woman, and before she even said hello, she was sending me on an errand.

"More tea?" I said.

Her friend held her glass high. "Me too."

Two more of her friends extended their glasses to me. Then a few more. Dewey and I took seven foam cups in total to the tea coolers and filled them. When we returned, we introduced ourselves.

The girl wore a baby-blue blouse and brunette hair pulled back. I noticed her plate was mounding. She had so much fried chicken she had to remove her earrings before she started eating. I never saw a girl eat like that. Most girls I'd dated had been too afraid to eat in front of boys.

"Hey," I asked the girl, "how'd you sneak all those drumsticks past the Potluck Nazis?"

"Yeah," said Dewey. "You got more chicken than anyone else."

She laughed. "I told them my mother was in the hospital with shingles, and I was making her a plate to take home."

"Oh, that's horrible," Dewey said. "Is your mother gonna be okay?"

She laughed. "Yes. My mother's never had shingles."

This young woman handled her biscuit with two hands. She cleaned her chicken bones until they were ivory white. Then she used the remainder of her biscuit to scrub her plate in clockwise circles. She was opinionated, funny, happy, and spoke so fast I had to ask her to repeat most of her sentences.

When she finished eating, I marveled. I wasn't even halfway through my second drumstick, and Dewey hadn't even gotten to his pear salad yet.

"That was impressive," I said. "You ate faster than Dewey. Most Rottweilers can't eat faster than Dewey."

"It's a gift," she said. Then, she looked at my plate. "Are you finished with that bone?"

"Bone?"

"Yeah, there's a lotta meat left on that. Are you done?"

Without asking, the young woman gathered my bones into a large pile. She proceeded to remove the tendons with her front teeth like a grizzly bear cleaning the carcass of wild boar. When she finished with my bones, they sparkled.

"My name's Sean," I said.

The girl licked her fingers. She smiled. Her brown eyes danced. "My name's Jamie," she said. "I'd shake your hand, but my fingers are too greasy."

So we touched our elbows together instead.

And my life would never be the same.

CHAPTER 13

WHERE RIVER ENDS

 Our Floridian bay was calm, smooth, and full of evening activity beneath the surface. I skipped a rock on the water. I've always been an expert rock skipper. It's one of my rare talents.

A voice came from a window in the house behind me. "Almost ready!" It was a young woman's voice. "Five more minutes!"

"Take your time!" I hollered back.

I skipped a few more rocks.

Our bay is the love child of Alabama's Choctawhatchee River and the Florida Panhandle. The bay sits in Florida, fed by the Choctawhatchee, which is not a huge river. Its two wandering forks cross the Alabama line and stitch the two states together so that you can't tell where Florida begins and Alabama ends. Eventually the river gathers itself into 129 miles of surface area we call heaven. And if you've ever seen it, you know why.

The bay of my youth is adorned with a choir of southern pine, beech, magnolia, laurel oak, Florida maple, and longleaf. The big water attracts birds from all parts: Canada geese, redhead ducks, American bald eagles, egrets, and majestic blue herons.

Feral hogs have been roaming these forests since Hernando de Soto accidentally left his hogpen gate open in 1539.

Here, there are old timers who still remember when the US mail was delivered by a boat trolling the shoreline.

Great manatees the size of Buicks linger beneath the water. Two-hundred-pound prehistoric Gulf sturgeons still feed on the basin floor like they have been doing since before Adam lost his rib.

This bay has a strange magic over a man. I have seen it bewitch those who have never seen it before. It's not to be under-estimated. I've seen this water capsize sailboats, uproot piers, and demolish cabins. But I have also watched it bless those who cherish it. I have seen it reward novice anglers with more bounty than they deserved and bring good luck to men who needed it.

This water has a spirit of its own, and if you're willing, it will love you. A man can find himself on a bay like this. I did.

And it was right here where I found Jamie Martin.

Her family had moved to Florida from Alabama. They had a modest brick home on the bay with a few trucks parked in the driveway and a crooked wooden pier shooting from the backyard into the gray water.

"I'm ready!" I heard Jamie's voice say.

She trotted out of the house wearing a pink blouse, jeans, and boots. Her voice was Alabama, her eyes were chocolate, and when I looked at her, I felt I had knowledge of her already inside me, tucked in a memory I hadn't touched yet. She was animated, and sometimes outspoken, but easy to love.

I'd never been so warmed by a person's company.

"Where're we going tonight?" she asked.

"I don't know."

"You hungry?"

"I could eat."

"Let's just drive around and look for a place then."

"Suits me."

We went driving. It seemed like that was always what she wanted to do. She didn't want to see movies, she didn't want dinner reservations, and she didn't even want to listen to the radio. She wanted me to drive. She wanted to place her bare feet on the dashboard with the windows rolled down and talk until her voice went raw. So that's what we did.

That night I burned through an entire tank of gas, riding the shoreline of the bay in grand circles, looking for a restaurant that suited our fancy. I took her through Choctaw Beach, Niceville, Valparaiso, Shalimar, Fort Walton Beach, and Destin until we ended up where we had started.

"I'm not even all that hungry," she finally admitted.

"Me neither," I said.

So we kept driving. We drove into Freeport to see the sun descend, making the sky gold and orange. Then we crawled into the truck and drove until we were on a series of dirt roads that circled the water. We came to a place where the secluded road forked, a place I'd never been.

"Which way do we go?" I asked.

"Don't care," she said. "Just as long as we stay near the water."

There's a metaphor here. I'm not sure what it is, but I don't have to know. Not as long as we stay near the water.

There was something about this girl that was almost child-like. She gave me the feeling you get when you are playing make-believe as a child. The excitement that comes with being the Lone Ranger, riding across the Sierra, chasing bank robbers, waving your cap gun. That sounds silly, I know. But she made me feel that way.

The road spit us onto a muddy beach. The sun was completing its descent, and the stars came out over the water. It was a violet sky, illuminated by a million planets above us. We sat on a patch of sand, close together, shoulder touching shoulder, and I could feel her. Not just see her.

When she spoke, it was like listening to a song I knew by heart. I couldn't shake the feeling that I knew what she was going to say next.

The pace of our conversation moved in familiar cadence. It was our own style. We developed it. It's ours. And it was as though we were resuming some ancient exchange we'd had before. We talked across the highpoints of our lives. And the low points.

She had her heart broken once; I never had mine sewn together. She had confidence that made her strong; I needed some. She was born in October; I was born in December. She liked milk chocolate; I liked dark.

And when the sun began to rise over Walton County, Florida, we were exhausted. We were no longer saying much but speaking in three-word sentences.

Then, it happened. This girl fell asleep against me, her boots removed, head against my chest. We held hands. I could feel her pulse in the palm of her hand.

I knew I would ask her to be with me forever, not because I couldn't live without her but because I wouldn't.

I was interrupted by a splash in the distance. It did nothing to wake the girl, but it caught my attention.

I saw a shape swooping from the dark sky. I saw broad wings and a craned neck, shaped like an S.

The dark bird glided above the water and landed on a rock a hundred yards from me. The thing stood still, looking straight at me. Its silhouette, lit by the moonlight. And I remembered someone I had tried to forget.

Why couldn't he leave me the hell alone? Why did his shadow have to cross every scene in my life? Why?

My father lost his right to be a spectator in my life a long time ago when he pulled a trigger. The last thing I wanted was his presence during the quiet moments with this woman.

The girl stirred. She pointed. "Hey, do you see that?" she said, sitting up. "Isn't he beautiful?"

Something came over me. I found a rock. I hurled it in the bird's direction. I missed. The rock made a splash in the water. The bird leapt from its perch and disappeared into the sky.

"What'd you do that for?" said the girl.

"He was getting too close to us."

CHAPTER 14

RED MAN

The greatest day of my life began with a barbecue sandwich. A good one. The sandwich featured a bun the size of an SEC regulation football and slow-cooked pork that tasted exactly like cherubs singing Handel. I sat on my tailgate, staring at the bay. The trees surrounded me. The sandwich stained my shirt with brown sauce and grease.

I would be married before sundown.

I looked into my rearview mirror to congratulate the old boy. I had barbecue sauce in my beard. My red hair was out of control. I used the grease from my hands to tame it.

I am a barbecue fanatic. If you were to cut me open, you would notice that my blood looks an awfully lot like KC Masterpiece, original style.

I eat when I get nervous. The more nervous I become, the more I eat. When I was a little boy, I once got so nervous before playing a baseball game that I ate nine drumsticks—a record I have yet to break. During the fourth inning I had to be escorted off the field on a stretcher.

I saw a man in a boat, skating along the bay. Even though it was December, he was fishing in a short-sleeved shirt. I recognized him. It was Ben, who used to live next door to my mother.

His wife had died a few years earlier, and it had nearly ruined the old man.

I had always liked him. He was soft spoken and kind, and he talked about the way things used to be. His wife, Barb, was a happy woman. They had a small house, two children.

When she got sick, his hair was brown. For two years, half the town prayed for her around the clock. You couldn't visit a supper table without hearing Barb's name mentioned. But Barb only got worse. And one day, the church bulletin announced that she had died.

I clocked out of work early to attend her visitation. The church was packed. Ben's hair was white. When I hugged Ben, I could tell there was something wrong. He couldn't remember people's names or recall how he knew them. The past two years of caregiving had worn him to a nub.

I waved. "Hey, Ben!"

He took his cap off and waved it, but he never said my name in response. I wondered if he remembered me or if he was just being nice.

"It's awful cold!" I shouted.

"I don't get cold!" he said. "I got Cajun blood!"

There were so many emotions inside me I couldn't pick one to feel entirely. There would only be three people in attendance on my side of the chapel for the wedding. Maybe four. This embarrassed me.

My future wife had hundreds on her guest list—half of an entire town. I didn't have enough people to form a basketball team.

I suppose that on my wedding day what I wanted was a father. I wanted a grown man to slap me on the back and congratulate me, maybe even call me "son."

I wanted someone, anyone, to at least talk to me like men do, giving corny marriage advice that nobody actually uses, like:

"The happiest men don't have the best of anything. They
   make the best of everything."
Or: "Beauty fades, but thank the Lord, so will your
   eyesight."
Or: "Marriage is not two people giving 50 percent.
   Marriage is two people giving 150 percent and then
   racking up massive credit card debt together."
And my personal favorite: "Don't go to bed angry."

Why couldn't at least one person shake my hand and tell me
they were proud of me? Or tell me not to go to bed angry? Even
though I had already heard it a hundred times, nobody had ever
said it directly to me.

Over the years, I'd been to friends' weddings and heard
these phrases passed down from the white-haired high priests
of the family who speak in quiet voices.

But my mother's parents were dead, and my father's parents hadn't spoken to us since the day of his funeral. They were
an angry clan, and I never knew his parents, nor his brother
or sisters. Once, my sister had called my father's mother on
her birthday. She was nervous dialing the number. "My name's
Sarah," my sister said into the phone. "I'm John's daughter."
But the old woman was silent. Finally, the woman said, "I don't
remember any Sarahs." My sister began to cry so hard that she
almost dropped the receiver.

After my barbecue sandwich, I reached into my jacket and
removed a pouch of Red Man chew. I don't chew tobacco, but
it had been a gift from my friend Will, who had first given me
two cigars. I don't smoke either.

"What're these for?" I said to Will the night before my wedding. "You know I don't smoke."

"Go ahead, sniff 'em," he said. "That's what you're supposed
to do with real fancy ones."

"Are these fancy?"

"The fanciest. I got them at Walgreens for a buck apiece."

They smelled like a litterbox.

"Thanks," I said. "But no thanks."

"Gimme those," he said. "You're a hick, you know that? An ungrateful hick."

The next morning, a packet of Red Man chewing tobacco showed up on my doorstep. A card was attached, which read: "For my favorite hick. Congratulations."

Will wasn't a close friend, but he was a friend. And like any upstanding male constituent, he wasn't going to let me spend my wedding day without a tobacco product.

Tobacco chewing is part of my family history. It was a rite of passage in my father's eyes. The first time I chewed, I sat on my father's truck hood, overlooking a moss-covered pond. Daddy gave me a pinch of brown leaves and said, "Whatever you do, don't swallow your spit, boy."

The chaw burned my mouth. I got so dizzy I almost passed out. And I loved it. Not the dizziness, not the tobacco, but I loved that he considered me a man.

"You don't really *chew* it," Daddy explained. "You just let it sorta sit there and spit a lot."

"Like this?" I said, spitting.

"Close, but spit farther. You're getting it all over my truck for cryin' out loud."

I spit hard. My head was seven thousand miles above the mesosphere. I thought I might puke.

My father must've been holding his laughter in because he never even smirked. He only gave approving looks even though I must have looked like a genuine dipstick that afternoon.

I remember he patted my back and said, "You're one step closer to being a man."

"I am?"

"Sure. Why, if you can handle chew, you're practically grown."

"If I'm a man now, can I have a beer?"

"Of course you can. Did you bring any?"

"No."

"Guess we'll have to wait several years then."

He fuzzed my hair. I was a *man*—at least in my father's eyes. I paid close attention to him. When he spit, I spit. When he sniffed his nose, I sniffed. And eventually, I vomited all over the ground.

My father didn't laugh. Men don't laugh at each other during serious rites of passage. Daddy only patted my back and said, "You breathe one word of this to your mother and I'll rewrite the will."

For hours after that experience, my head was numb, my eyes were hazy, and it felt like a goat had wiped his feet on my tongue. But this was the price of admission into manhood. All that was left was belching the National Anthem before a NASCAR race and eating steak tartare with my bare hands.

That's what Red Man Chew made me think of. The man I both loved and disliked. And when I spit brown spit into the bay water, the familiar dizziness came back to me.

Old man Ben eased his boat close to shore. He held a rod in his hands.

"What're they biting on, Mister Ben?" I hollered.

"If I knew that," Ben shouted, "I'd be home by now."

He held up an old-style wicker basket with a leather strap. It was empty. "Ain't caught nothing but a Mountain Dew bottle and a frog." Then he squinted at me. "What was your name again?"

Poor Ben.

"We used'a be neighbors, a long time ago. I'm Sean."

He slapped his knee. "Oh yeah! How's your sister?"

"Tall."

"And your mama?"

"Still short."

Silence passed between us. I watched the old man toss his lure into the water and yank it backward in the way men have been doing since the beginning of time. My highest aspiration is to one day become an old man.

"So what're you up to today?" Ben asked. "You here to fish?"

"No sir," I said. "I'm getting married today."

"*Married?*"

"I'm just enjoying my last few moments as a free man."

His face lit up. And even from far away, I could see his blue eyes were shining.

Then he guided his boat onto the sandy shore. He hobbled out and walked toward me. He looked older than I remembered. He was not a strong man like he'd been once; he was withered, covered in wrinkles and liver spots. When he reached me, he crawled onto my tailgate beside me. He was out of breath for several minutes thereafter, holding his stomach. We observed the December bay together in quiet.

"Did you know this is my bay?" he finally said. "My daddy gave it to me when I was ten years old."

"That's funny," I said. "I thought it was mine. My mother gave it to me."

"Is that right?" he said. "Well, I don't mind sharing. How's sixty-forty sound?"

"I can live with that."

He placed an arm around my shoulder. "Do you love her?"

The thought of this girl filled me with smiles. I could think of nothing more I wanted than to do the same for her.

"More than I love this bay," I said.

He grinned. "Well, then I got something I wanna tell you, something my daddy told me on the day of my wedding. Are you listening to me?"

"Yessir."

"No matter what happens in this life, no matter how bad things get, even if it looks like the sky is falling and there is no hope, don't ever go to bed angry."

Thank God for small blessings.

CHAPTER 15

BOWTIES AND MOONSHINE

I showed up to my own wedding late. Which was only fitting for me.

Since childhood, my mother had always said, "I swear, child, you'll show up to your own funeral thirty minutes late."

Which is probably true. Of course, I hadn't *meant* to be late. And in fact, I made it on time. But I realized I'd forgotten my rental tux and my rental shoes, so I had to turn around. I sped to my mother's house. In my bedroom I found the tux on a hanger and a Ziplock on my bed. The bag contained my bow tie, cummerbund, cufflinks, and lucky red baseball socks.

I drove to the chapel ignoring every stop sign, traffic light, and innocent pedestrian.

When I neared the church, I saw the parking lot full of vehicles. Cars spilled out of the parking area, onto the church lawn, and onto the road. Some were parked in the ditches. My uncle had parked his RV beside the playground swing set. Cars stretched backward to the county line, and more headlights were waiting to get in.

These were Jamie's people, from Brewton. They came by the hundreds and swallowed our little chapel like honeybees. In my truck, I bypassed the line of cars at the entrance by driving across the church lawn. My tires kicked up chunks of Baptist sod behind me. I skidded into a parking space and jumped out of the truck. My feet were bare.

My uncle stood on the curb looking at his watch. "We were beginning to think you'd had cold feet," he said. "You scared us all."

My future father-in-law came jogging toward me. He was a short man, with a jolly red glow on his face. "Thank God, you're here. I almost formed a search party with dogs and everything."

My uncle took the Ziplock bag from my hands and dumped it on the pavement. The two men rifled through the contents and got to work making me look pretty.

I slid on my lucky socks while my uncle adjusted my vest. My future father-in-law secured a bowtie around my neck while the usher placed cufflinks on my sleeves, and my wife's cousin waved a lint roller over me.

"Are those baseball socks?" said my father-in-law.

"Yeah," I said. "They're good luck. I won the regional championship in these things a long time ago."

"They smell like roadkill. When was the last time you washed 'em?"

"Fifth grade."

It's bad luck to wash lucky socks.

When the men finished dressing me, I felt like I was wearing a straightjacket. I stood tall for their inspection. They brushed my shoulders, fixed my hair, and wiped smudges of barbecue sauce from my cheek.

"You look good enough to eat," my uncle said. "But where're your shoes?"

Shoes.

Oh no.

I collapsed on the curb and buried my face in my hands.

"What's wrong?" my uncle asked.

This couldn't be happening to me. Not today, of all days. "They're on my desk!" I said.

"On your *what*? You're joking. You mean to tell me you forgot your own shoes?"

"Calm down," said my father-in-law-to-be. "Don't you have *anything* you can wear?"

I opened my truck toolbox. All I had were a pair of white rubber fishing boots. I put them on my feet and tucked my trousers into them.

"You can't wear those!" shouted my uncle. "Not unless you plan on carrying a five-gallon bucket and a cast net down the aisle."

"Hey, I've got an idea," my father-in-law announced, removing his shoes. "You can wear mine."

"Put those back on," said my uncle. "You have Barbie feet. Your tiny shoes will never fit his big feet. Quick, someone go inside and find someone with feet as big as his."

"What size are you?" said my father-in-law.

"Twelve and a half," I said.

My father-in-law disappeared into the chapel. A few moments later, he returned with a man who bore a striking resemblance to Herman Munster, with feet like industrial barges. The man had to duck when he came through the doorway. He removed his shoes.

"What size are you, sir?" said my father-in-law.

"Sixteen," said the man.

So I placed the pontoons on my feet and laced them as tight as they would go.

My uncle almost wet his pants. "He can't wear those things. He looks like Tickles the Clown."

"He don't have a choice," said my father-in-law. "We're outta time."

They escorted me into the church with careful steps, trying not to lift my feet too much. I moved with as much grace as a cross-country skier journeying across a frozen tundra.

The minister was waiting for me at the door. Before I joined him, my father-in-law pulled me aside one more time. He spit into his hand and fixed my hair. He stared at me in the face long and hard. He tucked a few folded hundred-dollar bills into my pocket and touched my cheek. "You're a good boy, you hear me?"

Which is Alabamian for "I love you."

My lips started quivering.

"Don't cry," he said. Then he smacked my shoulders. "You're one of mine now." Then he started crying.

Next, my uncle came to me. He hugged me hard, looked me square in the face, and in a reverent voice said, "Make sure you leave before sunrise tomorrow morning—you wanna make *good time.*"

I joined the minister at the altar. When the organ played, the audience stood, the doors to the chapel were flung open, and there she was, the rest of my life in a dress. Her hair was dark; her skin was milk. She walked the aisle with her father. She was the image of everything I have ever needed. Beauty, kindness, honesty, and humor. Always humor. And I belonged to her.

The minister asked who gave the woman away. My father-in-law shouted, "Her mother and me!"

My bride hooked arms with me, and in a voice so sincere and true, she whispered, "What in God's name is on your feet?"

There has never been a day that outranked the one I just told you about. And I don't think there ever will be.

You were missed, Daddy.

CHAPTER 16

MELTED ICE CREAM

It only takes a few words to change your life. And for me, those words were "I do." Ever since I said them to my wife, the sky opened up, and my life became what I always knew it could be. Happiness was no longer a distant idea. It was real. It was in my living room.

Our first apartment was seven hundred square feet with a window unit AC that only worked on non-business days. In the living room there was the phantom smell of a retired jockstrap. And our kitchen had one electric burner that worked when you beat it with a skillet.

The paint on the apartment building had faded during the early seventies. Most of the siding was either bare-wood gray or mildew green.

There was a drainage pond behind our apartments, designed to look like a lake. It was rectangular and filled with a waterish substance. It was a glorified ditch, and when the wind was just right, it smelled like egg salad.

The elderly man who lived in the apartment next to us was in a wheelchair. He had six family members living with him in his one-bedroom unit. He once admitted to me that they were stealing his disability checks. Still, they were nice people, even the friendly young man with the tattoo of a snake on his face.

The woman across the hall had two children who practically raised themselves—the kids even taught me how to play blackjack.

And the man in the unit above us had cats that roamed the property like a herd of sheep.

So this was married life. It was not fancy living, but it was heaven to me. I learned that love could paint over my world, in the same way grief had, but in reverse.

Our apartment complex came alive on weekends. Late at night, the women from Building L, dressed in short dresses and tall heels, would leave their apartments to go for a stroll around town. Once I asked our maintenance man, Jimmy Danny, about these women. He told me they were street evangelists.

Jimmy Danny weighed a buck-twenty and rode around on a dilapidated golf cart all day. He spent his afternoons changing lightbulbs, painting the lines of the parking lot, and fixing air conditioners.

There were a lot of fistfights in our complex. Jimmy Danny was in charge of keeping the neighborhood peaceful. This usually meant he would hurl himself between two flailing men, and sooner or later, Jimmy Danny would get slugged.

But since Jimmy Danny wasn't exactly the Sunday-school type, he hadn't heard about turning the other cheek, so he always hit them back.

On any given weekend, you could watch the show. The guy from 2A, who had six cellphones, a Porsche, and a girlfriend who—how do I put this?—was appreciated by many, would come to blows with a big man named "Tater Chip," who resembled a Pontiac.

But I didn't get to watch many fistfights. Saturday evenings were reserved for playing music. I played music with my friends at every smoky establishment from Mobile to Chiefland. We kept late hours and earned terrible money. The next morning, I would wake up at 4:00 a.m. and head to the Baptist church to play for Sunday service. The church paid me a hundred bucks per week.

During the daytimes, I hung tin roofing. But work was getting slow, and it was becoming hard to stay above water on such meager pay. Finally, the roofing company laid me off, and we were surviving on savings and the hundred dollars I got from church.

Things got tight. Our apartment needed a new air conditioner, for instance, but we learned to get along without one. On particularly hot days, my wife and I took turns sitting before the open refrigerator with our pants off.

We needed a new car too. My wife drove an ancient Oldsmobile that was on its last leg. She had inherited this vehicle from her mother. It was algae green, with one-hundred-percent genuine duct-tape upholstery, and the vehicle itself took up four lanes of traffic. To crank the engine, the car had to be put in neutral and pushed across the parking lot by three able-bodied men while someone sat behind the wheel pumping the gas, turning the key, and praying the Rosary.

Things got even worse, financially speaking, on the day the pastor fired me. The conversation went like this.

"I love you, Sean, you know that, right?"

"Right," I said.

"And I'd do anything for you, you know that, right?"

"Right."

"Good."

He rocked back and forth on his heels. I could tell he was uncomfortable.

"Is there something you need to tell me, Pastor?"

"Yes."

"Is it bad news?"

"Well, yes."

"I'm not fired, am I?"

"Well . . . I don't like to use that word."

"What word would you rather use?"

"We'd like to encourage you to use your talents on a volunteer basis, so you can reap an even greater reward in the kingdom."

I was devastated, but I understood. The church had to make cutbacks because of finances. It was a hard economy. Everyone was hurting. And the pastor's mission trips to Hawaii didn't exactly pay for themselves.

Even so, I kept attending services, playing piano at the church for free. I couldn't bear the thought of the sweet elderly folks singing without me.

It was a terrible way to start a marriage, but it didn't faze me. I was too happy to be affected by money matters.

I looked for jobs all over town with no success. Nobody was hiring. And even if they had been, nobody wanted to hire a high school dropout.

I'll never forget when I applied to be a telemarketer. The man sat across the desk from me and eyed the paper application I handed him. He frowned and stroked his chin.

"Lemme get this straight," he said. "You didn't go to *high school*?"

"No sir."

"Can I be honest with you?"

"Sure."

"We need someone who *sounds* intelligent over the phone. We need someone who at least graduated high school."

"You sell magazines."

"You're not hearing me, son. What I'm saying is, we're looking for more experience."

"I might not have gone to high school, but I've read a lot of books."

"Good luck to you, son."

"With very big words in them."

"I'm sorry, son. I can't hire a dropout. My boss wouldn't like it."

He showed me the door.

And, well, it only takes a few words to crush you. I walked out of that interview feeling like a waste of cosmic space. Old feelings of failure came back to me by the metric ton.

Yet I wasn't giving up. I went to a few more places, filling out more paper applications. I dropped my rural accent and tried to speak like a Harvard grad, pronouncing my *I*'s with all my heart.

Eventually, I found myself in an all-you-can-eat seafood joint, begging the manager for a job as a server.

"Sorry," said the manager. "We don't need servers. It's an all-you-can-eat *buffet*. People serve themselves here."

"How about a cook?" I said.

"Don't need cooks. Got too many as it is."

"I'll wash dishes."

"Already got dishwashers too."

"Please," I begged him. "I have five kids at home."

"Oh yeah?" he said. "Lemme see their pictures."

"Let you see what?"

"Well, anyone who has five kids to feed surely has a few photos in their wallet."

"Thanks for your time, sir."

The next day, one of the guys in my band told me his little sister was the manager of an ice cream shop. He pulled a few strings, and I got an interview across town. The joint was in a strip mall. My buddy's sister looked like she was twelve. She smacked her bubble gum and called everyone "dude."

She gave me one look and said, "You don't want this job, dude. No guys ever want this job."

"What do you mean?" I asked. "Why not?"

"What I mean is, *dudes* don't usually wanna wear the uniform."

"What's wrong with the uniform?"

"It's pink."

I told her I didn't care if the uniform was a Speedo and a pair of chaps. I needed a job. And I was hired.

The uniform was indeed pink. Also, management dictated that employees were required to wear a pink sun visor. The serving apron had ruffles on the edges and an embroidered teddy bear on the chest.

My first day of work at the ice cream shop couldn't have fallen on a worse day, the anniversary of my father's death. It was like fate was playing an ugly joke on me.

The worst days of my life often occur on September 11 (Daddy's birthday) and September 14 (the day he died). No matter what I do, I cannot make these calendar days into good ones. They are doomed to be black and sad.

One year, on the ten-year anniversary of his death, my truck died on the interstate. I had to spend the night in it.

Another year, I wrecked a lawnmower while working on a landscaping crew. That happened on September 14. In fact, I woke up that morning almost expecting it to happen.

One year, on September 11, my wife knocked her own tooth out trying to pull start a Weed Eater.

And on this particular September night, I was dressed like a Care Bear, serving hordes of people who were all nice enough to compliment my visor.

It was a bad day, but money was money. And I really would've worn those chaps if they'd told me to.

Anyway, just before closing time that night, I was serving a group of teenagers who couldn't decide between Apple Dumpling and Cinnamon Mocha. The bell on the front door rang, and I saw a couple walk through the door.

My day went from bad to worse. It was a familiar face. A girl. Someone whose mother had once told me I'd never amount to beans. The girl was with a tall man who had devastatingly broad shoulders, a square jaw, and teeth so white he looked like the risen Savior. Mary held his arm. They laughed. They kissed. They were dressed like they'd come from a nice dinner. And in those moments before I was recognized, I thought about what I would say to Mary when she gave me that dreaded look of surprise.

But I kept coming up short. No matter what I would've said, there were no magic words that could've saved me from humiliation. She would take one look at me, laugh, and remember she once dated a boy who ended up in a Strawberry Shortcake outfit.

Mary and James Bond observed the chalkboard menu above my head.

I swallowed my pride and approached them. "Can I help you?" I said from behind the sneeze guard.

"Yes." The young man smiled at me. "We'd like to try a sample of the Triple Fudge Turtle Surprise."

"Coming right up," I said.

I waited for drama to unfold. I waited for Mary to gasp and an old-timey organ to play horror-movie music. But nothing happened.

I served their samples on miniature spoons.

"Nope," said Mary. "Too much chocolate. I think it's *definitely* possible to have too much of a good thing, don't you, sweetie?"

"I absolutely concur," said Bond.

Mary looked straight at me. Her eyes bore a hole into my forehead. Here it came. I waited for it. It was going to hurt.

She said, "I'll take a sample of Va-Va Vanilla."

I was dumbfounded. I gave them samples and wondered why she hadn't said anything. They licked spoons and conferred among themselves.

"Nope," said her friend. "Not enough depth, lacks body. What do you think, darling?"

"Totally agree," said Mary.

Gag me.

They sampled a hundred different flavors until it was well after closing time. They finally settled on Amaretto and Cocoa Bonanza with Butterfinger and chocolate chips. They left a fifty-cent tip in my jar. They walked away, arm in arm.

And Mary never said a word to me. The girl never even looked twice. I could see it in her eyes; she hadn't known it was me.

I had been fully prepared to feel bad when she recognized me. But I had not been prepared to feel so pathetic that I was unrecognizable.

I clocked out of work that night. I sat beside our drainage pond, overlooking our swamp. Why was I so sad? I was living the greatest days of my life. I was married to a beautiful woman who loved me. We had our entire lives before us, and vehicles that worked—most of the time. I was supposed to feel invincible, like all married men feel. But I couldn't seem to feel that way.

A fist fight broke out behind me. Next, I heard Jimmy Danny's voice hollering. I heard the sounds of a struggle. I heard Jimmy Danny howl in pain. I heard the other fellas howl even louder when they got theirs. I heard cuss words. And a little while later, there were blue lights and a crowd of onlookers.

When the police left, Jimmy Danny took a seat beside me on the bench near the pond. He was beat up and breathing heavy, holding a rag over his face.

"I think that idiot broke my nose," he said. "Can you believe that?" He removed the rag. "Does my nose look broken?"

I looked at it. "How do I know if it's broken?"

"Does it look all catawampus?"

"No."

He touched it and winced. "Yep, it's broken." Then Jimmy Danny pointed to my apron. "Why're you dressed like Betty Crocker?"

"It's for my job."

"Jobs," he spat. "Who needs 'em."

"I do."

"I hate this job—I'm through after tonight. I'm tired of always getting beat up for other people's problems. I'm putting in my notice tomorrow. I can't do this gig no more."

"Where will you go?"

He smiled. He was missing more teeth than I'd noticed. "Oh, I've been thinking about it a lot lately. I'm gonna go to college."

"College?"

"You dang right."

"You?"

"Who else?"

"Isn't it expensive?"

"Yeah, but so is being poor."

"What will you study?" I asked.

"Don't care. I'm getting legit. If my brother can do it, so can I." Then he walked away, holding his nose.

I was left staring at that drainage ditch, thinking long and hard about the date on the calendar. The aftereffects of my father's life and death had stolen things from me, but I had sat on my hands and let them vanish. I realized it wasn't his fault. None of my problems were the result of John Dietrich. He hadn't been around to give me problems. The only person standing in my way was me.

No more. I was finished being Sean the Loser.

"College," I whispered to myself. "By God, I'm going to college."

Like I said, it only takes a few words to change your life.

CHAPTER 17

BIG MAN ON CAMPUS

 I stood before the admissions desk of the community
college. It was an average office space with drab carpet,
lots of cubicles, and harsh fluorescent lights. I don't know
who invented fluorescent lights, but I wished they wouldn't have.
Never in the history of civilization has any important event ever
been enhanced by the glow of sterile commercial lighting.

I despised fluorescent lights. They made me uncomfortable
and reminded me too much of a hospital. And I hate hospitals.
These putrid lights make me feel as though at any moment,
a doctor is going to emerge from a back room and say, "I've
got some exciting news, Sean. They're going to name a disease
after you."

The lights were humming a little. I twisted my cap in my
hands while I waited for someone to arrive at the main desk.

I don't know why I was nervous, but the ugly lighting only
made it worse, imparting the same mood often found in various
county prisons and psychiatric wards.

A woman slid behind the big desk. "We'll be with you
shortly, sir. We're pretty backed up today."

So I wandered to the waiting area, which was empty, except

for one middle-aged woman who was busy knitting. She was wiry, with hard features.

"What're you in for?" she asked in a baritone voice.

"Sorry?" I said.

"Why're you here?"

"I'm not sure."

"You're not sure *why* you're here?"

"I thought I was sure, but I'm having second thoughts. What about you?"

"I'm getting my transcripts. I'm transferring to nursing school. I've never been so happy, four long years, and I'm finally getting my shot at a career. Are you a student here?"

"No, ma'am, not yet."

"So you're enrolling?"

"Well, maybe. I don't know if they'll let me in."

She stopped knitting and patted my hand like any mother you've ever seen. "Course they will, sweetie. It's a *community* college. You're part of the community, ain't you?"

"I'm a dropout."

"So?" She kept knitting at a frenetic tempo. "Join the club. I quit in the ninth grade and had a daughter. That'll make you popular in a small town. I enrolled when I was forty-two, first woman in my family to ever go to college."

"Are you making a hat?" I asked.

She held her work upward. "It's a hat for my granddaughter."

I too came from men who didn't go to college. My father never attended. They tell me he barely completed high school. My mother told me that my father's high school years had been occupied by three activities. Drinking, getting into fights, and hangovers. He was a kid with a lot of anger inside him, and a lot of alcohol.

Still, my father was not aimless like I was. Nobody could ever call that man aimless. He worked too hard to ever be that way. The one burning ambition of my father's young life was to become a fighter pilot.

He had been transfixed with airplanes since infanthood. As a boy, he collected military aircraft posters and built model airplanes. Later in life, these same posters and miniature jets could be seen in his work shed, his garage, or on the interior walls of our barn.

Model bombers hung suspended by fishing line over his workbench, framed photos of F-14s in flight, World War II–era flight jackets hanging on the walls. He was an encyclopedia of aircraft knowledge. He could tell you the dimensions of a Grumman F-11 Tiger from memory and why the Messerschmitt was superior to its competitors.

Once, my father told me that when he was a young man, he almost got a tattoo of an A-10 Warthog imprinted on his hind parts. That way, he said, he would finally know what it felt like to ride an A-10 Warthog to work.

My mother told me that my father applied to pilot school when he was a young newlywed.

The nurse led him into an exam room lit by industrial fluorescent lights where he stripped down to his skivvies. He had his eyes examined, his tongue inspected, his reflexes tested with a rubber hammer. They asked him personal questions.

Then the doctor said something to my father in a quiet voice. Instead of responding to the doctor's question, my father answered, "How's that, doc?"

And that sealed his fate. My father was 80 percent deaf in his right ear—a series of childhood ear infections had nearly ruined his ears.

The doctor inspected Daddy's ear canals briefly and sent him away. And since military doctors aren't in the business of breaking bad news gently, my mother says the doc told my father, "You're never gonna be a pilot, kid."

It took two seconds for my father's aspiration to be smeared on the sidewalk. My mother said he collapsed to the ground and bawled.

Then he got drunk. That night was the first time Daddy ever hit her. And I know what you're thinking; my mother should have left him. And you're right. In fact, she's said this a thousand times. "I should've left that man," she has said. "I should've left him right then."

But love complicates things.

Besides, if she would've left him, you would be holding a different book in your hands right now. Perhaps one that's about how to live successfully on a low-carb diet. And you don't want to read about low-carb diets.

After that, my father gave up. He saw himself as a failure. He got a job at a shoe store. Then a printing press. He finally became a steelworker like his father and brother. And that was the end. His life path was set in stone. He would weld iron beams with an acetylene torch until he died.

He was very good at what he did, but it was the great disappointment of his life. He never wanted to be a steelworker; he never wanted to weld. He wanted to be airborne, and when a man has a taste in his heart for flying, there's nothing that can rid him of it.

I remember one afternoon watching my father clean his work truck. Both his truck and welding machine were covered in the red mud of dirt roads and big puddles.

A large plane flew overhead and made a loud noise.

My father turned off the hosepipe. He stared into the sky the same way a boy would do. Five more planes shot overhead. They were flying in V formation. He let his head tilt all the way back, almost like he was listening to a symphony. He closed his eyes, smiled, and kept his chin pointed upward. The vibrations of the jet engines sounded like they were tearing the fabric of the air apart.

"What kinda jets are those?" I asked.

"F/A-18s."

"How do you know?"

"Because those are the Blue Angels, son."

When the jets were gone, he was sniffing the breeze with his eyes closed. And I saw my father cry—something he rarely did. He didn't want me to see him like that, so he turned his back to me.

And it was that same night, in his garage he said to me, "Don't waste your life like I did, promise me that. My biggest regret is not going to school. I hate myself for not doing it. Promise me you'll go. Promise me."

I promised.

Three years later he died. That same year, I dropped out of the seventh grade. And I soon discovered what it meant to hate yourself for not doing something.

Even worse, I had this nagging feeling that my father was disappointed in me, and this made me hate him even more than I already did.

After all, how do you love someone who is always disappointed in you? Furthermore, why should I worry about disappointing a man who ruined our lives? In no way was he worried about disappointing me.

But you can't quit being someone's son, even after they die. You can't stop feeling their wants and wishes, still floating on the wind. You can't help but feel that you owe your father what you promised him.

My new friend in the waiting area patted my back. "You'll be fine. Try to relax. When you're done with school, you won't believe how proud you feel."

"Really?"

"Oh yeah," the lady said. "My mom came to my graduation last week and hugged me for like ten minutes without letting me go and kept saying, 'You did it, Marilyn.' She's almost eighty-three. Yeah, that felt pretty good."

I realized I was at this school for me, not him. I was here because I did not want to be standing in my driveway one day, staring at a sky filled with jets only to discover I had missed my own life. I wanted to feel like I had done something that I could be proud of.

"Mister Dietrich?" the woman behind the desk announced. "We can help you now."

I stood. My stomach was filled with acid.

My new friend winked at me.

I stepped toward the reception desk. I froze. What if I didn't have what it took? What if I really was stupid? I stopped walking. I almost turned and sprinted for the door. I don't know why. Maybe it was the fear of rejection. Or maybe it was the god-awful fluorescent lights. Either way, I felt ridiculous being there. I started to crumble fast.

The lady behind the desk said, "I'm not gonna bite you. Come here."

I couldn't seem to make myself move. I had no business in this room, I had no business doing anything but blue collar work—what in the name of Mike had I been thinking? This receptionist would probably laugh me right out of the building. I turned on my heel to leave.

"Wrong way," the receptionist said. "I'm over here."

I approached her. I rapped my hands on the counter and bit my lip. And for the life of me, I wish I would have said something a little more clever. But all I could get out was: "I wanna go to college, ma'am."

Spoken like a true hick.

"Well," she said. "You're in the right place for that. Did you bring your high school transcripts?"

There it was. My death sentence. I hung my head. I

considered leaving again and never coming back to Northwest Florida. I could run all the way to Mexico, change my name to Paulo, or Julio, or Chuchito, maybe start a new life making sandals out of recycled tires and selling them to Californian tourists.

"Well," I said. "I don't have any high school transcripts, ma'am."

It hurt to say. It hurt worse than I thought it would.

"But I promise, ma'am," I went on, "I'll do whatever it takes to get into this college. I'm a really hard worker."

Her face broke into a smile. "Don't you worry 'bout a thing, sweetheart. Why, if you wanna go to college, we're gonna get you into college even if we have to break the rules."

And for eleven years thereafter, I learned to love those fluorescent lights.

CHAPTER 18

FOOLS AND CHILDREN

 Mobile, Alabama. A bar and grill. Very little emphasis on "grill." Mobile is up the road from my house, only a few hours away. There are only two major cities near me. Pensacola and Mobile. I am here tonight with my band. We are playing music until the wee hours. Almost every weekend, we have been coming to Mobile to play for establishments like this.

I love it here. You should see this place. Live oaks surround the bar with limbs that twist in all directions, covered in moss, arching over an empty highway. These trees seem too wise to be so close to a rundown saloon like this, but they can't do anything about their plight. They can only grow where they are.

They are trees from an ancient world, and there is mystery to them that words do little to describe. They are older than the men who built this tavern. They will be here long after this place erodes into a heap of sand. And when the wind rushes through their leaves, you get the feeling these trees know all this somehow.

Parked beneath the trees are scores of trucks, sitting side by side like horses on the hitching post. Each vehicle bears a bumper sticker with a slogan like: "Gun control means using both hands." Or: "Four out of every three people have trouble with fractions."

Patrons smoke cigarettes. Most men wear caps with heavy equipment logos. A few wear cattleman hats. Quiet conversations are swallowed by the sounds of laughing.

Two women walk by a group of older men. The women are middle-aged, wearing tight-fitting jeans. The men are gray-haired. The old boys stand straight, suck in their bellies, and smile. One man opens the door for the women.

Every man wants to be noticed by a lovely young woman tonight. And every woman hopes to be noticed by a handsome young man. Too bad there are no lovely young women nor handsome men here. Only regular people.

My band had just finished playing a Hank Williams number entitled: "My Bucket's Got a Hole in It." People applauded half-heartedly. Over the microphone, I told the audience—if that's what you would call a roomful of people shouting over our music—that we'd be back in fifteen minutes. Nobody seemed to care whether we were.

I wish someone would've told me that the older you get, the faster time starts to move. When you're born, you are crawling on the slow-moving treadmill of life. In your teens, you're walking. By your thirties, you're running.

Adulthood overtakes you. It's incremental. You lose track of speed and forget all about your age. Soon you realize you've been in college for nearly a decade.

That was me. After leaving job sites, I would screech into a college parking lot, change my dirty shirt, apply deodorant, eat a peanut butter sandwich, and write a five-hundred-word essay with a pencil. Then I would sprint into class, leaving a trail of notebook paper behind me. And I loved every minute of it.

I read Hemingway, Steinbeck, and Twain. And I fell in love with O. Henry and Flannery O'Connor. And I fell in love with education.

After my last evening class, I would rush back to my truck.

I would change my clothes again, speed to Mobile, and play at some joint that smelled bad. These are the places I would spend my nights. Music paid more than installing floors, and strumming a guitar was more fun than operating radial saws. And eventually, I was playing more music than I was operating power tools.

I was almost thirty, and I was still scrawny, with messy red hair that never laid down. I would've rather been at home with my wife, eating pizza, watching past episodes of *The Andy Griffith Show*. But this gig paid two hundred bucks. And two hundred bucks was two hundred bucks. Besides, my wife wasn't at home. She cooked for a living. And working in a commercial kitchen is not a day job—it's a life job. My wife spent years before a stove, obsessing over the correct temperature of beef.

Our little four-piece band played anything you wanted to hear. We were not a great band, and we never rehearsed. We simply showed up, shook hands, plugged in, and earned our money.

That night, I sat at the bar on my break, overlooking a math textbook. I hadn't slept a full night in two presidential administrations. I had mid-terms bright and early the next morning.

"Beer?" said the bartender, Willie, who everyone called Williford.

Willie was six foot four, stocky, and a woman. I once saw her lift an average-sized man over her head, spin him like a helicopter, and throw him ten feet. She married that man a few months later.

"No beer," I said. "I've got midterms in the morning. Got a three-hour drive home tonight."

"Mid-terms? I didn't know you were in college," Willie said with a big grin.

"Well, I *won't* be after this semester is finished."

"Congratulations. I remember what that was like. It's a good feeling to finally be done."

"You went to college? I didn't know that. I'm envious. What's your degree in?"

"Nuclear physics."

"I'll just take a coffee, Willie."

The man beside me scooted closer. He patted the bar and said, "Put this young man's coffee on my bill."

I turned to see a man who was looking at his glass, not at me. He was older, with broad shoulders and a long, skinny neck. He wore denim and boots. He had auburn hair and a sharp nose. He looked like a cross between Roy Rogers and Mickey Mantle.

He sipped his beer. Then faced me. "How many years did it take you?"

"Eleven."

"Are you a postgrad?"

"Nope, Baptist."

He raised a glass. "Here's to you, son. You finished."

This man wasn't just a look-alike. He was a talk-alike. He was an act-alike. Even his mannerisms were replicas of a Kansan I once knew. I wanted to ask him where he was from and what he was doing there, but a bigger part of me wanted to leave and have nothing to do with this man.

"You know," he said, "I've been looking at you all night. Have we met before?"

His face showed years on it. His skin looked like a roadmap, and his eyes looked like they'd seen everything at least once.

"No," I said.

He shrugged and then presented his hand. "Jake's the name. But people call me Jay Jay."

"I can pay for my own coffee, Jay Jay." And I ignored his hand.

I took the small stage again. My band played songs you've heard a hundred times. I played songs a man who once loved me appreciated. Willie Nelson, Merle Haggard, and Hank Senior. There was a crowd, but I didn't see them. I only saw that strange man with the skinny neck. He dropped a fifty into the tip bucket.

"Good luck with your midterms," he said. Then he left the place.

The guys in the band grinned at each other over the tip. Dewey got so excited he nearly offered to give the man a piggy-back ride home. But I was too numb to be impressed. I saw the man sidle out of the joint with a familiar gait, and I didn't care if he got hit by a truck on a lonesome highway.

But when he disappeared, those feelings disappeared with him. I realized I didn't want him to leave. Not yet.

I chased after him. I shot through the front doors and saw a truck, blinker flashing, about to turn onto the desolate highway. I raced toward the vehicle and caught up with it. I rapped on the window. I was out of breath, my legs hurting.

"Wait!" I said. "I was lying."

He only smiled. "Come again?"

"I lied. You *do* look familiar."

He threw his gear shift into park. "Really? I *knew* it. Maybe I knew your old man."

"Yeah, maybe."

Neither of us said anything after that.

When I looked at him closeup, I felt foolish. He was not a look-alike at all. He was just a stranger with a lean neck, nothing more. Maybe my mind was playing tricks on me. Maybe I was losing my grip on reality. Or maybe sometimes you see what you want to see.

Even so, I didn't want him to leave. I didn't want to forget his face. He looked enough like the man I knew to satisfy something inside me. I wanted this stranger to leap out of that truck, to transform himself into the spirit of a dead man, and to tell me he missed me. I wanted him to tell me how sorry he was. I wanted him to swing me in circles like he did when I was a boy. I wanted him to kiss my hair and tell me he loved me.

"I'm a fool," I said. And it was all I could say.

"Yeah, well, my mama always said that God watches over fools and children."

"My father was John Dietrich."

He shook his head. "Doesn't ring a bell," he said.

We pumped hands. He drove away. I stood upon the yellow lines of a quiet rural highway, somewhere in the night of Alabama, looking upward at gnarled tree branches.

"Bye, Daddy," I said.

Something hard within me began to thaw.

CHAPTER 19

GIRLS BECOME WOMEN

Her name was Ellie Mae, and she was a gift from my wife. When Jamie brought the animal home, the dog was nothing but legs, ears, and stink. We were instant friends. And after our initial meeting, we rarely stood more than six feet apart.

She spent the afternoons in my passenger seat, head hanging out an open window, waiting for me to finish class. She accompanied me to job sites, and she even crossed state lines with me to play music. On this particular day, she was joining me for a wedding. My sister's wedding.

I steered the truck with my knees, and I tucked my shirt in to my pants.

My sister had been very clear about the condition of my shirt when she'd given instructions.

"Wear a *nice* shirt," she demanded, "or I'll murder you with a pitchfork."

"Oh c'mon," I said. "What's that supposed to mean?"

"It means that I will be carrying a pitchfork in my trunk."

I screeched into the parking lot. I told Ellie Mae to wait in the truck. I kissed her goodbye. She kissed me back. A long string of snot-like drool found its way onto my clean shirt.

"Oh, no!" I said. "Look what you did, Ellie!"

She blinked.

I tried to wipe the drool with a rag, but as it turned out, the rag was oily. It got black dog hair and motor-oil-colored smudges on the white fabric. Then Ellie Mae tried to lick the stain to make things better.

Time was wasting. I gave up and jogged through the courthouse, looking for a group of people in pastel-colored clothes, holding bouquets. I saw them gathered near tall columns, glancing at their watches.

"You're late," my wife whispered.

"Traffic got crazy," I said.

"Your sister was freaking out."

"My sister always freaks out."

"What happened to your shirt? Did you kill a hog?"

The ceremony was a success, as far as weddings go. My mother was crying, my wife was sniffing beside me, and everyone was smiling so big we had sore cheeks.

It was an emotional flash flood. When the preacher moved his mouth, I heard no words. I was stuck in a hayfield, with my baby sister riding on my shoulders. A girl who always had red cheeks. She tried to run away from home once. She was going far away from our broken lives and starting over. But I talked her into staying and giving our family another chance.

Here was the little girl who needed me nearby so that she could fall asleep. The girl who had a weakness for feral dogs and once told me she believed she had mental powers and could make her enemies explode simply by concentrating. She colored pictures for me when I was away at work. She rode on my hip until she was old enough to vote.

"Who gives this *woman* away?" the preacher said. His words were loud and clear.

He was calling her a woman. This was all wrong. She was

not a woman. She was my sister. My heart moved sideways in my chest. This wasn't a phrase I'd ever expected to be aimed at me.

I realized there was a girl attached to my arm. Who was this? I didn't recognize her white dress or her smooth skin. She looked straight at me. Her hair was dishwater. Her cheeks still had a reddish look to them, like a child who spent too long playing outside in the cold.

The preacher cleared his throat. "Who gives this woman away?"

My father should've been the one responding. But he'd left the job to me.

"Her mother and I," I said.

It was not right. Her service should've been in a huge chapel, with hundreds of people in tuxedos and evening gowns. She deserved a reception in a ballroom, with big cakes, a loud band, obnoxious groomsmen, and bridesmaids who danced and giggled too much. That's what she deserved. What she got was a brother on lunch break, whose dog was waiting in the truck.

When the ceremony came to a close, my mother asked me to pray aloud for everyone. This took me by surprise.

"Pray for what?" I asked.

"Just say a prayer for everyone." Then she pinched my side so hard she drew blood.

Never have I felt so underqualified. I swallowed the brick in my throat and felt everyone staring. It had been years since my last prayer.

"Go on," my mother said.

People dropped their heads and closed their eyes.

And . . .

I couldn't think of anything to say. Zip. Zero. Nada. My sister opened her eyes. She looked like she was about to use the pitchfork. My mother pinched me again.

My lip started quivering. I became choked. I didn't mean to, but sometimes things just swell within you and you are powerless against your own feelings. My mother squeezed my arm. Eyes closed. She said, "Sssshhh," the same way she's been doing since the day of my birth.

I was making a mockery of myself. Then something inside me started to crack—a dam I had built long ago to protect myself from a man who wasn't even real anymore. I still couldn't speak.

And I thought about him. Only it wasn't him I saw in my mind. Instead, I saw the face of the man from the beer joint, a stranger who I had actually touched. I remembered how it felt to shake his rough hand. I remembered the smell of his truck cab.

Finally, everyone said an uncomfortable amen.

My sister kissed her husband. And it was all over so quickly I hardly remember it well enough to write about it. My sister and her spouse crawled into his Toyota, and she waved at us from behind the passenger window. If there's ever been a human who was more ecstatic than my sister was, I wouldn't believe it.

My mother wrapped her arm around mine. "Are you okay?" she asked.

"I'm fine, Mama. I'm sorry I made a fool of myself."

"Don't be silly." She kissed my forehead. "You remember what your daddy used to say: 'God watches over fools and children.'"

CHAPTER 20

VISITING THE DEAD

 Five in the morning. I was lying in bed beside my wife with a ninety-pound bloodhound between us. My home phone rang. The telephone had a high-pitched ring that vibrated the utensils in our drawers.

My wife punched me. Not lightly. She nailed me in the mouth. I screamed.

When a man gets married, he thinks he's marrying a woman. But he's not. He's actually marrying four women at once. He is marrying:

1. his wife,
2. his wife when she's hungry,
3. his wife when she's hormonal, and
4. his wife when she's sleeping.

All four are stern women who can be mean enough to drive nails into oakwood using bare hands.

I learned this the hard way. I am not just married to Jamie. I am married to different versions of her. I had learned how to handle these incarnations of my wife, but none was as terrifying as Sleep Jamie. You do not want to meet Sleep Jamie in a dark alley.

148

Awake Jamie is sweet, outgoing. She might say things like, "Can I make you some breakfast, sugar?"

And you might answer with: "How kind of you, dear. How can I ever repay you? I know! May I take out the trash for you?"

But during sleeping hours, she is transformed into the devil. Sleep Jamie has no regard for human life. Sleep Jamie could kill a man. Do not touch Sleep Jamie, or she will smack, kick, bite, and on one occasion—as in the case of the January of '04 incident—headbutt you. She will have no memory of this when she awakes; therefore, she will feel no guilt, which leads to repentance.

The phone rang again. Another punch from Sleep Jamie. This time to the left eye. Another ring. Uppercut to the kidneys.

I crawled out of bed, clinging to life, and answered the phone quietly, trying not to disturb the Yeti beside me.

"This better be the cops," were my first words. "And someone better be in the hospital."

An automated voice said, "Will you take a collect call from . . ." Then a high-pitched voice: "Dewey."

"Yes," I said.

"Morning," said my pal.

"This better be good."

"It is good. I'm about to be at your place with Krispy Kreme and coffee. Now hurry up and meet me downstairs. I have to go to work in thirty minutes."

I peeked through our curtains. "It's five in the morning."

"I know."

"Why did you call me *collect*?"

"Duh, 'cause I didn't have quarters. Besides, I didn't want to knock on the door—you know, Sleep Jamie and all."

"What's the emergency?"

"Maybe you didn't hear me. I said: 'Donuts.'"

"That's not an emergency."

"It is when they're hot."

"Dewey, you can't just wake me up at five in the morning and expect donuts to make everything all better."

"The box is so hot it's burning my hands."

"I don't care."

"Really? The Sean I know would do anything for a chocolate cake donut."

"Did you actually get chocolate cake donuts?"

"I can't believe you even asked."

I sighed. "How about crullers? I need at least one cruller if I'm coming downstairs in this cold weather."

"It's Ferris Cruller's Day Off, buddy."

I descended our steps. Ellie Mae followed close behind. In a few minutes, Dewey rolled into our parking lot and squealed into a parking space. Soon we were seated on the tailgate of his Bronco, two grown men licking vanilla glaze straight off our fingers.

It was a cool morning. The sun was rising over our drainage pond, reflecting on the surface of the raw sewage. If you looked at the big puddle just right, tilted your head, squinted your eyes, held your breath, and tried to stay positive, the water almost appeared beautiful.

My friend's vehicle was loaded with ladders, cables, and power tools. Dewey had been my friend for several years, but we were nothing alike. He was impulsive, irrational, and outspoken. I was thoughtful, careful, and a world-renowned genius.

He tossed Ellie Mae a donut. She caught it in her jaws and swallowed it. After she swallowed, she flashed him a wide-eyed look that is often accompanied by a Sarah McLachlan song on television.

"Please don't feed her donuts," I said. "They're not good for her."

"Don't be silly," said Dewey. "Donuts are good for everyone."

"I'm serious. I don't want her to get fat. She's already getting a little bottom heavy."

Ellie Mae resented this remark.

Dewey was a free spirit. He was five-foot-five, with cobby arms and a strong set of shoulders. He was a wind-up toy that someone had cranked too tight. Sometimes he played fiddle tunes so fast that nobody in the band could keep up. He smoked too much, and he was bad to drink.

He was there for a very specific reason that morning. Dewey wanted me to go on a road trip with him to visit his father's grave in Tennessee.

It was an odd request. We were not the sort of fellas who discussed our feelings. We were guys who belonged to the Men without Fathers Club. This club has chapters all over the world. Most members handle the dreaded subject of fathers by reverting to our corporate policy: never handle the dreaded subject of fathers.

We do not get into emotionally charged conversations involving family photographs, and we do not say things like, "How did that make you *feel?*"

His request hit me in the wrong area.

"Sorry, Dewey," I answered. "I'm just so busy with work and school. I couldn't leave."

"Please," said Dewey. "I'm begging you. There. Are you happy? I'm begging. I never thought I'd have to beg my friend to do anything."

"It's not a good time. I graduate this semester."

He hung his head. My friend looked like he'd lost fifty pounds. I didn't often see him look so defeated.

"Why now?" I asked. "I don't get it. I've never even heard you mention your father."

He was quiet. He wiped his fingers on his trousers. He didn't say anything for a few minutes. Sometimes a man doesn't have to say anything because words don't do the feelings justice.

Finally he said, "It was my daughter. She's the reason."

"So if you wanna go, go. You don't need me."

Ellie sat beside Dewey. With her eyes, she willed him to stroke her head. This is a superpower all dogs have. Dewey petted her.

"I remember when I was five," said Dewey. "My dad came home from Arkansas, and he gave me this trumpet. I was like, 'What in the world did this old guy get me a trumpet for?'

"My dad said, 'Here, Dewey, found this in a flea market, reminded me of you.' I got so obsessed with that stupid trumpet that I practiced it almost every day. I got this book on how to play trumpet, how to hold your mouth and everything.

"By middle school I was the only kid in the fifth grade who knew how to play an instrument. I just wanted him to come back one day and see me playing that trumpet and say, 'Hey, that's my boy.'"

More silence. Dewey and I were treading on brand-new territory. Until that day, the most emotional thing we'd ever discussed was the SEC National Championship.

"If *you* don't go with me," said Dewey, "I know I won't go because I'm a chicken."

"I'm honored you asked, but I just can't leave town right now. I'm too close to graduation."

He nodded. "I understand."

"When're you leaving?"

"Friday."

I patted his back. "Dewey, good luck."

"Yeah."

"I'd better get back upstairs before Sleep Jamie starts to wonder where I am and sets fire to the apartment."

"Right."

I started to walk away, but Ellie wouldn't leave his side, not even when I called her. So Dewey grabbed Ellie's collar and led her to me. I thanked him.

"Hey," he said. "Do you ever wonder if they're sorry?"

"Who?"

"Our dads, you know, for acting like jerks?"

The last thing I cared about was how my father was feeling. I felt vinegar in me. It was an ugly sentiment that I'm not proud of.

"Who really cares, Dewey?" I said. "There comes a time when a kid just has to be a man and grow up."

And I left him.

CHAPTER 21

TRAILER COURTS

 The sun was out; the crickets were hollering. A pretty morning can make even an ordinary trailer court look majestic. I rode through the lines of dilapidated mobile homes until I arrived at one that was brown and tan with a rusted roof and crooked shutters.

I stood on a small wooden porch attached to a single-wide trailer. The front lawn was overgrown and served as a habitat to three quarters of the snake population in Northwestern Florida.

I knocked on the door. Ellie Mae sat beside me, chewing on what looked like a used breast implant she had found in the yard.

A five-year-old girl answered. She was in a pink nightgown with messy hair. She smiled in that sleepy way children often do.

"Hi, Mister Sean," she said.

Ellie Mae wandered toward her, and the little girl giggled with delight.

"Margie, is your daddy home?"

Ellie licked her face and the girl cackled.

"Mister Sean," she said, "why're you carrying that huge bag?"

"Well, because I'm a fool who's about to do something he's going to regret. Don't ever be a fool, you hear me, Margie?"

"Yes."

"Promise me."

"Okay, I promise."

"Will you go get your daddy?"

In a few minutes, Dewey came to the door. When his eyes landed on my duffle bag, his face broke into a million pieces. Before I could speak to him, he body-slammed me and we embraced.

I peeled his arms back and said, "Listen to me. I have one condition. Are you listening?"

"I'm listening."

"Hold up your right hand and take an oath."

"Do what?"

"You want me to come with you or not?"

Dewey held up his hand.

I cleared my throat. "Do you, Dewey Middleton, agree to uphold the terms set forth on this day, by your friend, legally know as Sean Dietrich?"

"I do."

"Then repeat after me: I, Dewey Middleton . . ."

"I, Dewey Middleton . . ."

"Will at no time touch the steering wheel, unless Sean gives permission."

"Will at no time touch the steering wheel, unless Sean gives permission."

"And at no time will I, under any circumstances, touch the radio."

"And at no time will I, under any circumstances, touch the radio."

"And I will at *no time* take a drink of any alcoholic spirits, whatsoever."

"And will at no time touch the radio."

"This was a bad idea." I picked up my bag and started walking off the porch without looking back.

"Wait!" he hollered. "I was only kidding! Of course I promise. You know I don't drink much anymore."

He spit in his hand. We shook on it.

By noon, we were staring at mountains in the windshield. Ellie's head was hanging out the back window, cheeks flapping, ears blowing backward. She had never seen mountains before, and she seemed overwhelmed.

It's hard not to be overwhelmed. If you drive seven hours north from the Choctawhatchee Bay, all you see are the Alabamian mountains, which eventually usher you into the taller mountains of North Georgia and then Tennessee.

You'll pass sloped hayfields, rural remnants of an era gone by, filling stations, white clapboard churches, and hillsides swallowed in kudzu.

I once planted kudzu in my aunt's backyard as a practical joke. She never knew about it until five years later. One fateful summer, her yard became a dense jungle. Even her grill was covered. Three days later, I was voted out of the family.

Dewey sat in the passenger seat, sipping gas station coffee. I was wearing a buckskin cowboy hat, spitting sunflower seeds into a Styrofoam cup.

After nine hours, Dewey was holding a map sideways and tilting his head to read it. Without warning, he screamed, "Quick! Take that exit! *There! There! Turn now!* That's Highway 11!"

I veered as soon as he said it and almost flipped his Bronco. We rocketed into a ditch with the tailgate in the air. When we landed, Dewey was lying in the fetal position on the dashboard, sucking his thumb. Ellie Mae was on top of my head.

"Well, nobody can accuse you of being a *good* driver," said Dewey.

"How about a little advance warning next time?" I said.

"I don't remember agreeing to that in our verbal contract."

We managed to get the Bronco out of the ditch. Dewey's

bumper was twisted on one end, and one headlight was broken, but otherwise the truck was okay.

Soon we were rolling along Highway 11 through the tip of Georgia until we hit Tennessee. We passed shaggy barns, grain elevators, silos, pastures, and the ancient remnants of towns that had dried up. We finally arrived on a shallow mountain, driving the hairpin turns that led up toward the dome of the Volunteer State.

We stopped at a filling station, perched across from a peanut field that was on the side of a mountain. Dewey trotted inside to ask for directions. Ellie followed him for moral support.

I sat on the tailgate, eating a peanut butter sandwich. It was the first trip I'd taken in a long time. I rarely ever left the Florida-Alabama region. I removed my ten-gallon hat and dusted it off. I turned the hat upside down and unfolded the leather sweatband. In black handwriting the name *John Dietrich* was scribbled inside.

Long ago, when I was a boy, we lived in Tennessee, not far from Spring Hill. My father spent two years building the GM plant, a herculean factory made of steel and sheet metal. On his off days, I remember the hikes we would take through the Smokies. He would drive these same two-lane highways, eating sandwiches, listening to the radio at full-blast. And he would be wearing this very hat.

He loved mountains. All mountains. They had a strange power over him, and I guess that's why he wanted his remains to be scattered on one.

Dewey walked out of the filling station with a six-pack of Budweiser and a bag of Doritos. Ellie was carrying a bag of pork rinds in her mouth.

"We're close," Dewey said. "The guy told me the cemetery's just up the road a few miles."

He tossed beer into a cooler. He tore open his Doritos bag.

"Not so fast," I said. "You promised you wouldn't drink on this trip."

"I know."

"So what's the beer for?"

He shrugged.

And even though I didn't mean for them to, sharp words fell out of my mouth. They were words that had nothing to do with Dewey. This trip was bringing back thoughts I wasn't ready for.

"Dewey," I said, "this was a stupid idea. We should've never come."

I didn't even know why I'd said it. I still don't know. Who did I think I was? A man has a right to grieve his father however he wants, for as long as he chooses.

Dewey opened the bag of pork rinds for Ellie Mae and said, "I know it's stupid, but I still wanna go."

Suddenly I felt like a horse's rear. I apologized.

"Don't be sorry," he said. "I've thought the same thing a hundred times. In fact, I've tried to visit this dadgum mountain cemetery *three times*, and each time I chicken out before I ever get this far.

"But I'm just so tired of punishing him. I'm exhausted— from all the work it takes to keep hating him."

We crawled into the vehicle, and Ellie Mae jumped into the backseat. But I couldn't start the engine. I couldn't make my hands turn the ignition. I only rested my hands on the wheel.

"What's the matter?" he asked.

I handed him the keys.

"I think you oughta drive this part."

Dewey drove like a bat out of hell until we arrived at an ancient cemetery that had seen better days. I stepped out of the Bronco and almost lost my lunch from carsickness.

We explored the graves. The gray stones bore the pock-marks of age. The inscriptions were faded with years. The weeds had grown so tall you couldn't see anything but pasture in some places.

Dewey's mood changed when we arrived. He was on mission. He roamed the empty yard, Ellie Mae following with her nose to the ground. Together they inspected every headstone with the ferocity of coon hunters. I gave him plenty of distance because this is what men do for each other.

After almost an hour of searching, Dewey finally found a marker located in the corner of the graveyard, beneath a dead tree. And I knew he'd found the right grave when I saw him remove his cap.

I sat in the tall grass, minding my business. I turned the buckskin hat in my hands and inspected the writing in the hat band.

Finally, Dewey hollered at me from across the cemetery: "You wanna meet my dad?"

So, in the sunset of the Tennessee mountains, Dewey introduced me to his old man. He was not the friend I'd known for so long. Even though he was a grown man with children, a loving wife, and a forty-foot mansion on wheels, he looked young in the late afternoon. Maybe I did too. Maybe we were both children, not the men we thought we were.

"You know," said Dewey, "I never knew his real name. It's weird. Everyone always called him Jim, that's what I always heard them say. I just naturally thought his name was Jim, but it wasn't."

The sounds of cicadas swelled. The tall grass moved in the breeze. A droplet of water rolled off his nose and landed on the ground. Then another. And another.

The tombstone read: "Dewey James Middleton."

We stayed for a long time. A lot longer than we needed, but not as long as Dewey would've wanted. Before we left, my friend placed an unopened six-pack on his father's grave.

"All I ever wanted was to share a cold one with my father," he said. "That was all I ever wanted."

We drove home in one night. My friend slept the whole way home with a half-smile on his face.

I gazed at the mountains in the distance. I hated mountains. All mountains. Because mountains were him. They were what he loved. I didn't want to love what he loved. I didn't care if I ever climbed another rocky summit again. And I told this to the mountains. Out loud.

But the mountains weren't buying it.

CHAPTER 22

PRIVATE TUTORS

Eleven years. Eleven whole years.

Eleven years of working crummy jobs just to pay for college. Eleven years of eating suppers in my truck before class. Eleven years of leaving the campus early to play music at some joint for a lousy hundred bucks.

Eleven years of sleeping in my vehicle with my dog because I was too tired to drive back home. Eleven years of memorizing homemade flashcards containing information vital to a general degree, like which phylum Ommastrephidae squid belong to.

Eleven years of research papers and nights in the library trying to figure out whether the appropriate parentheses for a term paper are the square-looking ones [like these guys right here] or the curved ones (these little babies), and why the Modern Language Association (MLA) cares so much about them (because they suffer constipation). Also, why don't college professors allow the usage of curly-looking parentheses, because clearly they look much cooler than the plain ones {see what I mean?}?

Eleven years of turning in handwritten essays to uninterested professors who, before giving a grade, glanced at my work with the same sincerity it takes to scratch one's haunches.

Eleven years of trying to become proud of myself—which isn't something that happens overnight. Eleven years trying to make my mother proud. Eleven years trying to impress a man who only lived inside my memory.

And eleven long, squelching, torturous, demonic, heart-twisting, cruel and unusual, hellish years of math.

Without my wife, I could never have graduated. I wouldn't have even come close because of math. Math is one of those things the good Lord allowed on this earth to remind mankind that the devil is real. Only, the devil's name is not "Lucifer" like I once learned in Sunday school. His name is, in fact, "Big Al," which is short for "Algebra." Also, his wife, "Calc," is even more terrible than he is. But nobody is as bad as his three children, "Trig," "Stat," and "Cosine."

I am not good at math. In a perfect world, that wouldn't matter. After all, nobody uses trigonometry to do important things like make a ham sandwich, pay taxes, or raise a family. But colleges need to turn profits to stay afloat during difficult economic times. That's where math classes come in.

By requiring math courses, colleges milk the liberal arts student for a little more cash.

Colleges are kind of like cable TV companies.

Let's say you want ESPN so you can see the big game. So you call the cable company. You want the Silver Package, which is $14.99, the cheapest package they have, but as it turns out, this package only offers crummy channels nobody wants, like the Surgery Channel and the Twenty-Four-Hour Accordionists Network.

"But I just wanna watch the game," you explain to your qualified sales associate on the phone.

The cable representative points out that you can upgrade to the Gold Package for $64.99 and get popular channels like Vegan Cooking Channel, Total Racquetball TV, and the Ceramic Clown Figurine Network.

"But what about the game?" you ask.

"Sorry," the representative says. Then he goes on to tell you that for $304.99 you can get the Platinum Package which includes all the channels people care about.

"Three hundred bucks?" you shout. "All I want is the big game! Can't I just order ESPN?"

No, you can't, big boy, because that would be too easy. You can't just go around getting what you want in life without suffering for it.

Getting a college degree is like this. If you want one bad enough, you're going to have to buy the Twenty-Four-Hour Accordionists Network first.

But let's get back to math. Even if you wanted to get a degree in, say, Trench-Digging Science, you would need fourteen math courses, three organic chemistries, and at least four accredited hours in the dead languages of Norway.

The problem is that my brain doesn't do numbers. When someone starts talking about numbers, all I hear are mushy sounds that don't mean much. When I see numbers on a page, they might as well be Mandarin characters. And this, along with other reasons, is why it took me eleven years to finish school.

My wife, however, is a math genius. She tutored me on Monday and Wednesday nights and muscled me through each math course. It was a miracle we stayed married because teaching me requires an almost biblical amount of patience. Often, my wife would attempt to explain basic algebraic concepts only to realize her husband's numerical IQ was the same as that of a residential water heater.

During the evenings, my wife and I would sit at the dining table. My bloodhound would sit at my feet for encouragement. My wife would hold a book in her lap, glasses low on her nose, pencil behind her ear.

"*This*," she would explain, pointing to the page, "is the *negative* exponent. Can you say that?"

"Neg-a-*tive* exponent."

Ellie Mae barked in agreement.

"Right," my wife went on. "Now this means it's on the *wrong side* of the fraction, and *that* means, you need to *flip the base* to the *other side* of the equation in order to solve for *x*. Got it?"

"Got it. Flip the base."

More barking.

"Close," my wife said. "Flip the base to the *other side of the equation*. You can't just flip it, it has to go to the *other side*. Get it?"

"Got it. The other side, which would actually be the defense."

"No, there's no defense. These are *fractions*."

Bark! Bark! Bark!

"Right. I meant offense."

"Will you shut that dog up? It's very important that you understand this, or nothing else will make sense. Now try repeating it back to me."

I took a breath and closed my eyes. "Negative exponents are part of the offensive fractions, which are numbers *fractured* into miniature *algebraic shards* and placed on earth for the forgiveness of sins . . ."

Bark! Bark! Bark!

"Shut that dog up!" my wife would yell. "Now look at these numbers. These are *ex-ponents*. The *exponent* is the *little number*, which is a *quantity* representing a *power*, to which a *given number* is raised within the *mathematical expression*."

"That's your opinion."

"Okay, now say it back to me."

Bark! Bark! Bark!

"These numbers," I began, "sitting beside the base, are *ex-patriots*, who once dressed up like the *Cleveland Indians* and threw *all the tea in China* into the Boston Harbor, thereby winning the *Indy 500*."

And that's how I lost my left molar.

My wife doesn't have a superb sense of humor. But it doesn't matter because she has a wellspring of love that runs deeper than the core of this earth. It's because of her that I can even spell my name without getting nervous.

After eleven years of math, she prepared me for finals. This tedious endeavor took months of tutoring. We practiced solving equations until my eyes hurt. Then we practiced some more.

A lot was riding on these finals. Throughout my eleven years, even with her help, I had failed three math classes. Three. Math almost made me give up on school completely.

On the night before my big test, we stayed up until two in the morning, huddled over a large textbook, sipping the same kind of tea the Cleveland Indians once threw into the Boston Harbor.

The next morning, I visited my mother to change a lightbulb in her garage before class. When she answered her door, she gave me a funny look.

"What's wrong?" she asked. "Why do you look so tired?"

I told her I'd been up late, studying. I told her that in a few hours, I would most likely fail my finals, never graduate, and be doomed to hang drywall, lay tile, cut lawns, or work in bars until I finally died.

My mother knew how to give me a shot of confidence. She has always known how. She spoiled me with a large breakfast. Biscuits from scratch, a stack of bacon, eggs over easy fried in bacon grease, and grits with too much cheese. My mother knows the way to my heart, and this is why my doctor is concerned about my LDL and HDL.

I told her how badly I wanted to pass this class and how I wanted my degree. And she understood. My mother was the only college graduate of our family. When she was twenty-four, she put herself through school. She graduated with a Bachelor of Science and started working as a respiratory therapist.

She touched my hand and said, "I wanna show you something. Wait right here."

She left the room and rifled in a closet for several minutes. She returned with a small leather-bound journal. She opened it. The pages were filled with hand-drawn graphs, charts, and sine waves.

"What's this?" I asked.

"That's the Venturi Principle. These are things I had to study before I graduated, a long time ago."

I turned the page to see one long algebraic expression that took up three entire pages of the journal.

"That one was a tough one to memorize," she said. "But I still remember it, if you can believe it. I was always bad at math, but I worked hard, and do you know why?" She touched my cheek. "Because I knew I was smarter than I gave myself credit for."

"I'm stupid, Mama," I said. "Do you know how many times I've failed this class? More than anyone on campus."

And this was true. I had paid hundreds of dollars, and spent hundreds of hours on this singular godforsaken class, and I had only managed to prove to the world that I belonged in manual labor.

"You're *not* stupid," she said. "And I don't wanna hear you say that anymore."

Then she told me a story. It was a tale about a man. A man she doesn't often talk about. In fact, I don't think I had heard her talk about him much since he died. My father's name had been erased from our history books altogether. He was the great villain of our story, so we rarely referred to him.

But on this day, she drew back the curtain that separated us from him. And she told me about him, and she called him "John." A word I hadn't heard her use in a million years.

"A long time ago," she said, "I remember when John wanted

a promotion at work. It was so important to him because it was the difference between minimum wage and foreman's wage. That was a lot back in those days.

"But there was a problem. Daddy could hardly read the blueprints that foremen had to read. There was too much math involved, and oh, Daddy couldn't do math."

But my father was determined to learn. He was fed up with his current station in life, and he was going to show them all that he was just as smart as the next hick.

"Your daddy's friend Ben would come by after work and tutor him. You were just a baby back then, so you wouldn't remember. They'd stay up until the wee hours, looking at blueprints on the table, working all sorts of equations on notebooks. And Daddy worked like a dog."

She wiped the corner of her eye with her sleeve.

"I never saw John work so hard for anything. Nothing. But he wanted a better life for you and me, and he finally did it. If it weren't for all that studying, he would've never made one of the foremen over the GM plant in Tennessee, that was the biggest thing he ever did. Biggest thing he ever did in his life."

She stopped talking. She flashed me a weak smile. My mother rose from the table and left the room.

That morning, I drove across town to take my exam. In the classroom, I did a lot of deep breathing, and I almost prayed, except that I'd sworn it off a long time ago.

It took me two hours and nine minutes to finish. I was the last student in the room, and the teacher gave me ten extra minutes— just because. When I handed in my exam, the professor only glared at me. She'd seen me fail this class and set the all-time record for repeated Fs.

"How do you *think* you did?" she asked.

My shoulders sank. I thought I did awful.

"I *think* I'm probably gonna see you again next semester," I said.

"Is that so?"

"Yes, ma'am."

She smirked. "Do you know that I've failed a lot of students in my time?"

I could only imagine. This was a woman with the congenial personality of a fascist dictator.

"But," she went on, "I've never failed anyone *three* times in a row, and that really says something about you. I didn't expect to see you this semester, but you were here, you were never tardy, and that counts for something in my gradebook."

Then the woman flipped through the pages. She frowned. She shook her head a few times. I could see disappointment on her face.

I thanked her and started to leave the room.

"Mister Dietrich," she called to me. "You know that grades aren't to be posted for two weeks."

"Yes, ma'am."

"But I want to grade your test right now, so you don't have to wonder."

That night, when I arrived home, it was with slumped shoulders and a long face that resembled a bloodhound. My wife was standing on the porch, waiting. Ellie Mae was beside her, wagging her tail.

I stepped out of the truck and moseyed to the porch.

"Oh, no," my wife said. "What happened?"

Ellie Mae quit wagging.

I shook my head.

"There's always next semester," my wife said.

I handed her a packet of paper because I had no words to say. She looked at it briefly and then tossed it on the ground. We held each other.

"I can't believe it," she said. "You're a college graduate now."

CHAPTER 23

LATE MOURNING

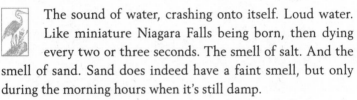 The sound of water, crashing onto itself. Loud water. Like miniature Niagara Falls being born, then dying every two or three seconds. The smell of salt. And the smell of sand. Sand does indeed have a faint smell, but only during the morning hours when it's still damp.

If I were a poet—and if you've read this far, you know without a doubt that I'm not—I would compose something about the Gulf of Mexico.

I've tried several times to no avail. My words come off about as poetic as a teenage boy trying to write a sonnet about a girl named Erica with red curly hair who doesn't know that the boy is alive and one day when he approaches her she tells him he looks a little bit like President Jimmy Carter in the face. Not that such a thing has ever happened to me.

If I wrote such a poem about the Gulf, I wouldn't write about the colors, nor the smell of the sand. I wouldn't write about the wildlife, nor the sea oats, nor the fine grass on the dunes, nor the way the foam gathers on the shoreline and makes you remember parts of your life you had forgotten. People have already written about those things.

No, I would write about its power. I would write something

about how my life—a life that has been lived out only a mile from this great and sometimes terrible creature—seems so small in comparison.

Still, no matter what circumstances I find myself tangled in, upon these shores of Northwest Florida, the Gulf uses its power to love me. How gentle the strength of the world's largest geographical mass. How kind.

I would also write about the sound. Not many people write about the aural pleasures of the Gulf. On a good day, you can stand beside the water's edge with your eyes closed and see forever. The crashing water is loud, rhythmic, and drowns out all thought. If you listen to it long enough, you get older in spirit, younger in body.

I'm not sure that last line made sense. See? I told you I'm no poet.

Jamie was out of town with her mother in Birmingham, visiting family. I was celebrating my graduation on the beach. I was camping with my dog.

I awoke to the wonderful, crashing sounds of water. But it wasn't the crashing sound that woke me. It was a soft dripping, like the sound of a leaky faucet. The fabric of my nylon tent had been collecting moisture on the inside surface while I slept. A steady drip had found its way inside. It was falling onto my pillow and upon my right eye. A puddle had formed in my eye socket so that when I opened my eyes I had the sensation that I was drowning. I yelped.

Ellie Mae leapt to her feet when she heard. Then she licked the water from my eye.

I took in a few deep breath of cold air. I could see steam clouds with each exhalation. I tapped my camping thermometer. The gauge had a layer of frost accumulated on the glass face.

"Sunny and warm in Florida," I said to Ellie Mae. "Yeah, right."

It was still dark on the beach outside my tent. I lit my propane lantern and hung it above my sleeping bag.

I dressed myself in wool socks and long underwear. It was still a few hours before sunrise. I made coffee over a small burner outside. I cooked a meager breakfast in an iron skillet beneath the stars. I made sausage, eggs, and grilled white bread. My dog ate the sausage and eggs; I ate the bread.

We listened to the tide move in and out.

Fort Pickens National Park is virgin coastline with white sand and emerald waters. There are no man-made structures visible for miles. No condominiums, no beach restaurants, no tiki huts, no jet-ski rentals, no cabana boys. The beach looks the same as it did when Ponce de León discovered Florida five hundred years ago.

The park has a state-of-the-art campground with space enough for hordes of diesel pusher RVs the size of eighteen-wheelers. However, some folks like me enjoy tent camping in the seclusion of the dunes.

Of course, this is illegal. You're not even supposed to walk on the dunes, let alone pitch a tent on them. But if you don't mind living on the edge, and your bloodhound has no moral objections, it's like being on the coast of a newly formed earth.

After breakfast, I scrubbed my skillet in the surf, using sand for abrasion. The water was so cold it stung my hands and made them numb. Ellie Mae sat behind me, watching the night sky. It was lit with stars that shined a little brighter than they did in other places on the map. It was like standing on the doorstep of heaven. The place where souls go, where goodness lives, where magic starts. Man, I really do wish I were a poet sometimes.

The water moved, and I listened to the whistling wind. And I didn't mean to feel something, but I felt it just the same. I fuzzed the hair of my bloodhound and felt so proud. It's not an emotion I often feel. I have often wished I could feel proud and confident, and I've even wished I could be cocky like other men. But I'm not any good at pretending to be that way. I never seem to have much to be proud about.

That morning, I was a different human being. I was proud as whitewash, but not the bad kind of pride.

Usually, when I thought about my ugly childhood, it only made me ashamed. I would sink into sadness when I thought about the marks my pitiful life left on me. I've told you about some of my story, but not all. I've touched on highlights and some low points, but I've left a lot unsaid out of respect for my mother.

But I felt no shame that day. I don't know if college did this to me or if it was the sound of the water.

I'll be honest with you. The variables that construct my existence are confusing, like handwritten math equations jammed together on a sloppy page of homework. They don't make any sense. One math problem leads to another. Then another. And so it goes. One day you realize that your life is one whole page of problems, and nothing ever gets solved—one ongoing equation with no equal sign at the end.

But it occurred to me, beneath the canopy of a starlit heaven, that I'd been looking at my life all wrong. It wasn't a math equation. Things weren't supposed to add up. There was no solution. In fact, there was no problem. Life's variables and numbers and pages of chicken scratch weren't mathematical marks. They were art. A drawing, an abstract painting. It was meant to be beautiful, not sensical. And embedded within the mess of it all were miracles. Small ones. I had never paid attention to them because I was too busy, but it didn't make them less real.

And I heard something behind me. At first, I thought it was my dog. But it was something else. It was the same noise you hear when you're making the bed, when you fling a bedsheet. Flapping.

I turned to see a shape against the moonlit sand. Its wings made a grand gesture. The old thing landed near me, close enough to touch. His legs were straight, his neck curved, his head poised. He stared at me for only a moment and then diverted his eyes. His mannerisms were dignified, calm. Maybe he was fishing. Maybe he was out for a walk. Or maybe it was something else.

The bird took two steps toward me and stared. And I was a child playing within the warmth of Camp Creek. I was a boy with reddish hair, too many freckles, and a crush on a girl who thought I bore a striking resemblance to the thirty-ninth president.

The bird caught a gust beneath its wings. It soared low first, hovering above the water. Then it rode the wind high above the world, and the old thing was gone. I don't know if it meant anything or not. But to me, it meant a lot. I don't know where it came from, but I knew which mountain it was going back to.

And when it got back to its Colorado perch, by God I would be there to greet it.

CHAPTER 24

OLD RED

 "Sorry," said the mechanic, kicking my tire. "This old truck won't handle that long of a trip. Sucker will probably break down soon as you get to Texas."

He was old, with paper-thin skin that wrinkled around his eyes. I didn't know if I could trust this man. A mechanic friend once told me that all mechanics were liars. Not just some mechanics, he clarified, but *all*.

"It's just in our blood," my friend once told me. "We can't help lying." And this, my friend claimed, was the reason for his first divorce. And his second.

I wondered if this man with oily hands was being honest. How can you tell if someone is concerned about your well-being or just wants your money?

"Gonna need new tires," the mechanic went on. "New brake pads, rotors, and I'd go ahead and get that AC fixed if you're going out West. My sister lives in Phoenix, and she can bake cookies on her dashboard."

"What's it gonna cost?" I asked.

He petted Ellie Mae and got grease all over her fur. Ellie resented this greatly because if a mess is being made, she likes to be the one who makes it.

"Cost?" he said. "Boy howdy, lemme think . . ."

He closed his eyes. The lines on his face became deeper. His eyebrows bunched together. He counted on his fingers but gave no answer. Instead, he looked inside my engine again. He touched worn belts. He unscrewed spark plugs, blew on them. He checked my windshield wipers, oil, transmission fluid, brake fluid, power steering fluid.

"At least a couple grand," he said. "I hate to break it to you, but I'm only being honest."

Whether he was or wasn't, I didn't have that kind of money lying around. And even if I *had* been able to scrape it together, I wouldn't be able to afford gas, food, or lodging after losing two grand. So that was that. My plan was ill-conceived. I didn't have the vehicle, the money, or the tires to visit my father.

Before the man walked away, he said, "What kinda business you got out West again?"

"It's a long story."

I shook the man's hand and thanked him for his time. He tried to pet my dog, but she wanted no more of his axle grease.

"Got kin out there or something?" he said.

"Sorta."

"Yeah?"

"Yeah."

This man was prying, but I didn't feel like talking. I was too disappointed.

This red truck had been with me for a long time. I'd taken it to nine states and replaced the tires when they started getting bald. The truck had been good to me. The rips in the seat cushions were old friends. The hairline cracks in the windshield, the chipped paint, the funny smell the heater made ever since the day I spilled a can of smoked oysters on my dashboard.

I patted the fender. Rust developed on the wheel well. I was proud of this rust. It had taken several years to mature into the good stuff. I had waited patiently for it, checking my truck every morning. We would never see the West.

Ellie Mae tried to console me. She could tell I was not myself.

I crawled into the driver's seat. I turned the key. The engine sputtered. I patted the dashboard and spoke sweetly to my truck.

"C'mon, Red. You can do it."

More sputtering. Hacking. Rumbling. Finally, the engine came to life like an eighty-year-old smoker walking up a flight of stairs.

"Atta girl."

Before I could throw the gear shift into reverse, I saw the mechanic standing at my window, blocking my way. His arms were crossed. I rolled down my window.

"I hate to pry," he said, "but I'm nosy, and if it's none of my business, just tell me to get lost, okay?"

"Okay."

"Why're you wanting to go out West?"

"I was going to visit my father," I said.

"Where's he live?"

"He doesn't."

He nodded once. "Oh, I see."

"That's why I was going. I haven't been to see him in a long, long time. Actually, I haven't been to see him at all."

"I'm sorry," he said.

"Thanks."

The man rubbed his chin. Then spit. I could see him thinking. He leaned toward me and cupped his hand over his mouth. He whispered, and his breath smelled strong enough to knock a buzzard off a manure wagon.

"I have an idea," he said. "But you would hafta swear you won't tell *nobody* about it, or I'll lose my job. Promise?"

"This was a strange man," I thought. I considered offering him a swig of Listerine.

"I don't understand," I said.

He glanced both directions. He removed a pencil from behind his ear. He scribbled something onto the back of a business card. He handed it to me. "This is my address and phone number," he said.

"What's this for?"

"You bring Old Red to my house, and my son and I can do the whole thing for probably four hundred bucks, maybe even cheaper if I get some used tires from a buddy."

I almost couldn't believe it. There was no way this could be happening. People simply don't go out of their way to help other people. Not in this world.

"You can't be serious," I said. "Why?"

"Who cares? Just bring it by the house, and bring four hundred bucks, and we got you covered."

"Earlier you said parts alone would cost more than four hundred."

"Don't you worry 'bout me. I got a buddy who gets parts cheap. It'd be a pleasure to help you. Besides, my son loves working on cars, and so do I. It'll be fun."

And I knew he was lying, of course, since all mechanics lie.

CHAPTER 25

LOS PLANOS

 The plains of Texas looked like a golden ocean of wheat and dust. They were dry and long and covered in wire-grass. There were old service stations perched on acres of brown and remnants of farms. Many stretches of highway were entirely surrounded by prairie. The familiarity of it all made me sick.

I was getting closer to Kansas. I wasn't sure I was doing the right thing by going. I had thought this trip would be one of self-discovery, like in the movies. I had wanted Jamie to go with me, but she believed it was something I needed to do on my own. And she was right. There are some things a man needs to do alone. Jamie sent me off with a cooler of chicken salad, pimento cheese, and a card that read:

> Remember to let the pimento cheese get to room tem-perature before you eat it. It's better that way. Don't forget to eat breakfast, it's the most important meal of the day. I miss you.
>
> I love you,
—Jamie

I wanted to see the places my father haunted, the barns where he'd baled hay, the places he'd lived. Then I wanted to travel west and visit his mountain grave. Actually, it wasn't that I *wanted* to go. It was more that I had to.

It was a grandiose idea. I see that now. But back then, I thought I could handle it. Now, I was finding out that I was wrong.

Ever since my mother left Kansas to be with her family in Georgia, she had vowed never to return. Thus I'd grown up without this state. We were Southerners. We didn't talk about Kansas, we didn't think about it, and we purged it from our minds. I was no more a Kansan than I was John Dietrich's son.

I wish it weren't this way, but I guess something happens to your mind when you go through trauma. The brain is altered forever in the span of only a few moments. You start to forget a lot.

It's funny, I can recall insignificant things with startling clarity, like tire swings and creeks and chickens roaming through the tall grass. But big things? No can do. I can't remember much. Not even when people describe these things in great detail. It's as though someone has wandered through my brain with a broom and dustpan and swept away most of my big memories, leaving only the tiny ones.

For instance, I can remember precisely the way my father would barbecue pork. In the churchyard, on a homemade cinder-block grill made with chain-link fencing. I remember the way the meat looked on my paper plate, staining the white paper red. I remember my father's pride over his barbecue.

But I have a hard time remembering what his face looked like, and sometimes I forget what his middle name was.

Jacob. It was Jacob.

How can a boy forget his father's face? How can he forget a name? Why did I have so many ugly feelings about a state?

The closer I got to Oklahoma, the more barbecue stands I saw. I pulled over at roadside barbecue stands galore.

Texas had good barbecue. Ellie and I stopped at three different joints to eat brisket in one day. The first place was a trailer in an abandoned parking lot of a Kmart. A woman stood beside a large smoker, stabbing a hunk of meat the size of a queen-sized mattress. When she saw Ellie, she gave my dog a piece of fat the size of a man's fist. Ellie ate it in two bites.

I ordered something, and the woman presented me with a plate of brisket—black bark on the outside, reddish on the inside—and only charged me two dollars. It was enough food to live on for six months.

I took one bite and moaned. It was some of the best stuff I've ever had. I asked for some barbecue sauce.

"Sauce?" she scoffed at me. "This is Texas, sweetie. We don't even use sauce on spaghetti."

Texans.

That night, my dog and I camped in a state park that was nothing but dirt and dry grass. The campsite cost nine dollars. There were no bathrooms or showers. The woman at the park entrance took my money and handed me a parking pass. Then she frowned and said, "Make sure you bury your constitution at least a foot deep, no less."

"My what?"

"Or else you'll attract the coyotes."

"I'm sorry, what are we talking about again, ma'am?"

"Bury hers too," she said, pointing to my dog. "Checkout's at noon. Have a nice day."

The wind got so strong that night that it felt like my tent would tip over. For a morning bath, Ellie Mae and I hiked to the Red River with a bar of Lava soap and a beach towel. I use the word *river* loosely because the widest part of the river was about as wide as a Snickers bar. I scrubbed in the water while Ellie Mae chased a jackrabbit that was wandering on the shore. She nearly caught the rabbit, but the rabbit called for reinforcements. Soon nearly eighty rabbits emerged from the brush and began chasing my dog across the Texas plains. These were not rabbits like we have in Florida. Some of these were carrying tomahawks, and a few were on horseback.

That day, we drove through wide prairies that were filled with tall, space-age-looking wind turbines. Multitudes of these machines went on for miles, peppering the prairie, looking like something from a cheap sci-fi movie.

The farther north we drove, the flatter the scenery became. The air was as dry as Prohibition, and the grass turned to wheat. When we hit the Oklahoma Panhandle, my stomach was getting sour. Even though it was sunny outside, it felt cloudy and dismal to me.

Even so, my truck had never driven better. After the mechanic had graciously outfitted it with second-hand tires, new AC, new brakes, and a miniature hula girl on my dashboard, it was like driving a brand-new vehicle. And the air conditioner hadn't blown air this cold since the construction of the Panama Canal.

We camped just outside the town of Elmwood, Oklahoma. I trespassed on private land. Actually, I wasn't entirely sure it was private property. I saw no evidence of civilization for miles, and I hadn't seen any posted signs or fence posts. It looked like we were in the middle of nowhere.

The weather was pleasant. We didn't need a tent that night. We slept on a foam pad and watched the stars come out to play.

When you travel, it's easy to get malnourished, so I tried to replenish our energy reserves by eating superfoods that were nutritious and full of vital minerals and vitamins. My dog ate a can of Spaghettios; I ate Doritos and a bag of gummy worms.

The plains of Kansas were looming in the distance, and they made the night feel unwelcoming. I wish I wasn't such a wimp, but I felt scared. The landscape reminded me of the man who had once belonged to this soil. And this reminded me of all he put us through. And this reminded me of the large black hole in my mind where Kansas used to be. Before I fell asleep, I heard the faint footsteps of tiny paws in the dirt. They were fast steps, accompanied by the sounds of sniffing noses. Ellie Mae whimpered.

"Who's there?" I shouted. I started to tremble so hard I almost couldn't speak in a clear voice. Irrational fears of childhood were coming back by the metric ton. Night terrors. Someone was going to murder me out here, and they'd never find my body.

More sounds. Footsteps.

Ellie Mae sat at attention.

"Hey!" I said. "Who's there?"

I saw eyes in the near distance, reflecting the light of our campfire. Coyotes probably. Or it could've been the war rabbits, returning for blood. There's not much of a difference between the two in the middle of the opaque Oklahoma night.

So my dog and I crawled into the bed of my truck and made our pallet there. I laid on the hard plastic liner holding my dog. I'm glad I had her with me, or I don't know what I would've done. I tried to forget about the predators around us. But there were more noises, and I was having vivid memories of things I never wanted to see again.

Finally, I sat up straight. I decided that I would do something about my fear instead of lying down and letting it consume me, like a big child who still wets the bed—which I have never done.

I reached into my toolbox and threw a wrench at the yellow eyes in the distance. The thing somersaulted through the air and hit nothing but dust. But it worked. I heard feet scurry away.

"Get back!" I said. "Or so help me! I'll . . . I'll do something really bad!"

What a tough guy.

That night, I couldn't sleep. I sat on the roof of my truck to make myself tall. When eyes came near, I aimed a flashlight into the darkness. Sometimes I could see the outlines of dogs.

I wasn't mad at my father anymore, and I didn't dislike him the way I used to. But I was still afraid of something. What, I don't know. I'm ashamed to admit that for most of my life, I've been afraid of things. I used to sleep with the door locked, and I would check that lock a hundred times throughout the night.

Maybe this is why I wasn't always a happy person. Throughout my life, some of my friends even thought I was sort of depressing. I was not like my peers. I did not possess the higher octaves of the human instrument. I was scared at night, I had bad dreams, I was afraid of strange people, I was quiet, I was lonely. Nobody tells you that grief feels just like fear.

But after graduating, that was changing. I had become a new me. I quit getting regular haircuts and sported a shaggier look. I spent more time with my dog, fishing, or playing music in various bands around town. I didn't want to be afraid anymore. I wanted to be me.

But I wasn't. And I could feel it that night. The farther from Florida I traveled, the less I felt like me. I was feeling trapped and threatened and fill in the blank. The closer I got to Kansas, the more I wanted to go back home to Florida and never return.

I saw a coyote walk into the light of my campfire, which smoldered. When I saw him, I could tell there was nothing to be afraid of. He was tiny and a lot leaner than I thought he'd be. His ribs showed, and his hair looked wiry. His ears were enormous compared to his slight head and long nose. I was surprised to find that he was not ugly, but beautiful.

Then he showed his teeth to me.

"Hell with this," I thought. I dug in my toolbox and found a two-liter Mountain Dew bottle. I chucked it into the distance and said a swear word. It bounced in the dust, and I saw the coyote run like the dickens.

I was disappointed in myself. I was becoming a scared little boy all over again. No longer was I the college graduate, swinging the world by the tail. I was a kid with trust issues. I was scared, I was alone, and I was without defense—unless you count the two-liter.

I was thirty-one years old, for crying out loud. What was I doing? Why was I visiting the ancient monument of a man whose face I couldn't even remember? He didn't deserve my respects. He was the reason I felt fear and sadness and inadequacy. He was the reason for everything bad in my life.

I heard a high-pitched howl from across dusty landscape, and it filled the night with song. Another coyote joined it. Then another. I must've been out of my mind, coming here.

"I hate you!" I shouted into the night.

I didn't mean to say it. I had meant to say, "Go away!" or "Get outta here!" But sometimes you end up telling the truth by accident.

I wanted to say more to whatever was out there in the dark. But I couldn't bring myself to say anything else. I just wanted to go home.

So that's exactly what I did.

CHAPTER 26

THE BOY COLUMNIST

It had been two years since my failed attempt to visit my father. The trip had embarrassed me so badly that I never told anyone about the failed pilgrimage until I wrote this book. As far as several people knew, it was a success. It is still somewhat of an embarrassment to me. Seeing it in print makes me feel like a fool.

Oh well. My mother always said that embarrassment is a good thing for a person. If that weren't true, she reasoned, then why are there so many karaoke bars?

Still, when I got back home from that trip, I felt like a moron. It changed me though. I made a few resolutions after setting my feet on home soil again. I resolved to forget my father for good. And for the most part, I kept my promise. I almost successfully forgot him altogether. And it wasn't out of spite. I wasn't forgetting him for bad reasons.

You see, my father has always been a kind of obsession for me. I have kept his grave memory around when I should've let him go a long time ago. I couldn't seem to control my thoughts of him. He was like a bad habit I couldn't quit. He was a foggy memory, but the bad things he did replayed in my mind like a VHS rewinding and repeating.

It seemed that whenever my mind would get quiet, I would think about him until it tormented me. Then I would wallow in my own sadness until I was muddy.

In some ways, I was a lot like an alcoholic who couldn't put down the thing that hurt him most. So one day I decided to quit the sauce. I would give up my father for good, not because I was angry, but because I was ready not to be.

"Forget the bad things about him," I told myself, "and forget the good things about him too." I didn't do it out of resentment, but to become sober.

And it was during this new liberation that I started writing. After all, I had to do something with all the energy I had left over since I wasn't thinking of *him*.

Initially, I wrote on a yellow legal pad with a BIC pen. Then I dusted off the Lettera 32 typewriter my mother gave me for college reports. It was blue and needed WD-40 to get the keys working again. But the keys felt good beneath my fingers.

The first story I wrote was about fishing in the Choctawhatchee Bay. It was god-awful. It was so bad that all the flies pitched in to get the screen door fixed. How could I be such a bad writer but have so much fun writing?

The fishing story was 500 words and humorous. And when it was finished, I felt like I'd done something, even though it stunk. So I tossed it into the trash. Then I wrote the same story again, by memory. This time, I included a few lines about my mother and about the hard life we had growing up. I talked about throwing the newspapers and about the way we leaned on each other.

The new story was 560 words. It was garbage, but it was better. I tossed it into the trash, and I wrote it again. It was 700 words. This time, the story was more about our lives and less about fishing.

I marked the story with a red pen and then retyped it for a

third time. Now the sucker was 920 words. The entire three-page, double-spaced story didn't even mention a fishing rod. It was about our lives, tossing newspapers, and about a trip to Oklahoma. The story was still awful, but at least it was heartfelt.

Soon I was writing every morning for two or three hours. Over time, this became five or six hours. And some days, I would write all day until my eyes were blurry and my ears rang from the sounds of keys hitting a platen.

Almost every time I sat behind that typewriter, I would try to write about something humorous or of local interest, but it would always get transformed into something about the fractured lives we lived when I was growing up. I found that the act of writing was like exhaling after holding my breath for a hundred years.

God knows, there are more educated men out there, and there are brilliant minds with more important things to write about. But you'd be hard pressed to find many men who are more screwed up than me. And that is why I write.

I began writing my short stories in newspaper-column form. Ever since the days of throwing a newspaper, I had wanted to be a columnist. There seemed to be importance placed upon the words of columnists and journalists, a sort that novelists are never granted.

Novelists and columnists are about as different as could be. Novelists spend years producing one perfect work; columnists have to produce work four or five times per week.

In a year, a novelist might produce a 400-page literary masterpiece. In that same year, a columnist will have already written almost 400 columns. The columnist doesn't have the luxury of overthinking his stories or heavily editing his words. There was something about this that appealed to me.

It is like the difference between a jazz pianist and a classical composer. A composer could spend years writing a symphony that a listener will hear as one hour of well-constructed music. A jazz pianist, however, plays piano, composing on the spot for three hours. His music is sloppy, honest, and unedited, but it's real. And that's what columns are to me.

After a few months, I had written nearly one hundred columns, but I had never shown them to anyone. So I started submitting my work to newspapers all over the Southeast. It was gutsy, but I was ready. I was met with some rejection letters, but most newspapers wouldn't even write back. They had bigger things to worry about than some guy with a typewriter.

But I kept writing, and I don't know why, to tell you the truth. I wrote about everything. I wrote about common people. Anyone who seemed to hide in the recesses of the world, who never received any limelight, who rose early to pack their lunch, who clocked out late. I wrote about my coworkers on jobsites, men who could pull electrical wire and mud drywall joints. I wrote about the worn-out waitresses at the establishments where my band played. I wrote about my mother, about my sister, about my wife, about my dog. And once, I wrote an entire column about ear hair.

I did not write about my father.

And when I finally got a letter back from a large newspaper in Georgia, I almost wet my pants. They asked me to come for an interview. That same week, I drove six hours north. I even bought myself a necktie. Soon I was on a sidewalk beneath a tall building with mirror-like windows stretching toward the sky.

"Wish me luck," I said to Ellie, who sat in the passenger seat, working the lid off a jar of Jif with her jaws.

I leapt out, carrying a manila envelope beneath my arm. I took a few steadying breaths and chanted, "This is crazy, this is crazy, this is crazy . . ."

I arrived in a lobby. I waited in a big leather chair. Old feelings of underconfidence returned. The receptionist called me into the office. It was the biggest office I've ever seen. It had a large picture window, and there were M&Ms in a bowl on the desk. I waited in a chair that was three inches off the floor. I ate so many M&Ms they colored my organs.

Finally, a woman in a pantsuit walked into the room. She had white hair and red-rimmed glasses like Sally Jessy Raphael. She shook my hand harder than most pipefitters I've known.

"Let's make this quick," were her first words. "I have a lot to do today."

I handed her my envelope. The woman didn't look at it. She tossed it on the desk and said, "Where'd you study journalism?"

I almost made a puddle in my khakis. "I went to community college, ma'am, and I didn't study journalism."

"Okay, what'd you study then? Are you an English major at least?"

Oh boy.

"Well, I have, sorta, a liberal arts degree, you could say, ma'am."

She opened my envelope and looked at the pages. She looked like she could use more fiber in her diet. "You wrote these on a typewriter?" she asked.

"Yes ma'am."

"We use computers. Do you know how to use a computer?"

I was beginning to feel like a real hick now. Of course I knew *how* to use a computer. What kind of a patronizing question was that? I had an AOL email address that I checked well over twice per year.

She scanned one of my stories, crossed her legs, and clicked her teeth. The woman shook her head. "I'm sorry. We could never run something like this. People don't wanna read this kinda stuff."

The woman seemed to be waiting for me to say something, but I had nothing to say. I was still trying with all my heart and soul to remember my AOL password.

"I'm gonna level with you," she said. "I got journalism majors lining up around the corner. Some just wanna be interns and work for free. I need someone who knows what they're doing."

It was a hard pill to swallow, but I took the medicine. I thanked her for her time. When I started to leave, the woman must have rediscovered that tiny, almost undetectable, itty-bitty sliver of a human heart she had, because she said, "Wait! I'll make you a deal. You find me a good story, maybe we'll talk."

It's funny how much power you give people over you. Her disappointment in me had lowered me into the pits of hell. But her last remarks made me feel as though I were being nominated for an Academy Award.

I raced down the stairwell to my truck. I was sweating by the time I reached the sidewalk. I called my wife on the phone and told her about the meeting.

"You'll never believe it!" I shouted. "She told me if I can find a good story, we would talk!"

"So what're you gonna do?" my wife asked.

"I don't know, but I'm gonna get that woman a story if it kills me."

The first thing I did was eat barbecue. I have always found that barbecue helps the human body work better. The cholesterol lubricates the mental passages. I asked the waitress at the barbecue joint to bring me the yellow pages.

"I don't know if we have one," she said. "Can't you just look it up on your phone?"

People like me didn't have fancy phones with internet access. My cellular phone was a clamshell phone with an LCD screen.

I called each nursing home in the area and asked one question: "Do you have someone in your nursing home with a good story?"

Most of the replies were something like: "Everyone's got a good story in here."

But I was looking for something more. I finally reached one nurse who said, "We got a lady here with the best story you ever heard."

The woman was pushing ninety. Or maybe she was pulling it. The nursing home was all the way in Jasper, Georgia.

I asked the nurse, "If I come today, could I have a meeting with this woman?"

The nurse said, "Don't see why not, but you gotta hurry. She takes chair yoga at six."

I glanced at my watch. There was still plenty of time. I tipped my waitress and drove until I hit Jasper. The nurse buzzed me through the doors and shook my hand. She had arranged a meeting with the old woman.

The nurse led me to the rec room, which was littered with board games and puzzles. I sat at a table with a notepad and a pen. A white-haired woman came shuffling into the room.

"Are you with the IRS?" the woman asked in a gruff voice. "I already paid what I owe."

"No, ma'am," I said, standing to my feet. "I'm with the newspaper."

It was only a half-lie.

"Really?" she said. "The newspaper wants to see me? What for?"

"We heard you have good stories."

The woman's face lit up like a flame. She sat across from me and asked, "You wanna hear my story?"

"If you'd be so kind," I said.

"Are you kidding? I've been trying to get someone to write my story for years." Then she hollered, "Nurse! Nurse!"

The nurse appeared and asked what was wrong.

Miss Margaret smiled at the nurse—I am not making this up—and shouted, "Get me a Miller Lite!"

"Yes, Miss Margaret," the nurse said.

"Hold on," the old woman added. She looked at me. "Do you want a Miller Lite too?"

"I do."

Miss Margaret took a sip and explained: "I've been drinking beer since I was twelve. The doctor said it was good for an ulcer I had, and so my mother would bring me beer with every dinner. Just one. It's a habit I have always kept up."

And there in Jasper, Georgia, an elderly woman spoke for two hours straight without taking a single breath. She recounted her entire life to me. I didn't even take notes. I only listened. She told me about her childhood, her adulthood, her children, her late husband, and her golden years.

It was an epic. Her husband had died when she was in her twenties and left her with four children to support. She took a job as a custodian in a local school and earned her GED when she was in her thirties. After that, she went to college. She taught high school until she was in her late sixties. When her story ended, my beer was long since finished, and I had fallen in love with a woman sixty years older than me.

Her story was a little bit of my story, wrapped up in pieces of my mother's story, and I felt like we were family somehow. There was something about this meeting that touched me so deeply. I have not been able to shake the feeling it left me with. I still feel it today.

I thanked Miss Margaret and gave her my number. I jogged to my truck and told my dog all about what had happened. She was not impressed. She was hungry.

I called my wife.

"How's it going?" she asked.

"I visited a nursing home today."

"Come again?"

"I made some wonderful friends there."

"You're scaring me."

"I drank beer with a woman who looks like Barbara Bush."

"Are you feeling okay?"

"Can't talk now, honey. I'll be here one more day, tops. I really think I can do this, Jamie. Gotta go now, I love you."

"Love you."

I camped at a KOA resort that night. I removed a typewriter and placed it on a picnic table. I typed 2,000 words about an old woman named Miss Margaret, and I wrote it like it was my own mother. And over the course of six hours, I whittled the story to 800 words. I fell asleep with a typewriter beside me and a dog huddled against my back.

The next morning, I felt exhausted, but gratified. I reread the finished copy of the story from the night before. "Not bad," I thought. I made a few marks with a red pen and retyped a final draft. Twice.

Then I drove into the city, this time without a necktie. I rode the elevator to one of the top floors and told the receptionist I wanted to see the editor.

"She's in a meeting," said the young woman.

"I'll wait," I said. "She's expecting me."

It was an hour before the editor invited me into her office. The woman seemed somewhat amused. She smirked and said, "Do you mean to tell me you went out and got a story *right after* you left?"

"Yes'm," I said.

"But, don't you live in Florida?"

"The Panhandle."

The woman was kind enough to read my work, all 800 words. When she finished, she frowned.

"Nope," she said. "I'm sorry, this won't work for us. I don't think you get it." The woman leaned onto her elbows. "I'm gonna give you some free advice that nobody ever gave me.

"Nobody wants to read stories that are about happy things.

That isn't how you sell books, newspapers, or magazines. People want things that are gut-wrenching. You've got to really change the way you think about writing. You can't just write goody-goody stuff and expect to make a living at it. We need more blood and guts, less romance. I'm sorry."

But something was different about me. I was unmoved by her words, and I'm not sure why. The lady had pretty much told me that I sucked eggs. But it didn't hurt. Because within those last twenty-four hours, I received my first taste of journalism, and I liked it. It was the first time in my entire life that I didn't feel like a construction worker, or a bar musician, or a screw-up. I was a writer, and I could feel it in my bones no matter what this lady said. Furthermore, no matter how correct she might have been, there was no turning back for me now.

I collected my papers and shook her hand with a firm grip.

She said, "It was a good effort, but I'm sorry."

I smiled at her. "I'm not."

CHAPTER 27

WORLD SERIES CHAMPS

 November. It was already getting cold in the Panhandle. I'm talking bone cold. Temperatures were sinking all the way to sixty-two degrees in some places.

My band was playing music that night. On breaks between musical sets, the band visited my truck, parked beside a dumpster. Ellie Mae was waiting in the passenger seat. The truck windows were rolled down, the keys were in the ignition, the radio was playing the World Series. A small crowd gathered around the truck cab to listen.

At the truck, I found four waiters, three dishwashers, one civilian, two fry cooks, and a hostess listening to the radio.

The dishwasher was a boy named Dane. He was fifteen, with red curly hair and freckles. He looked a lot like I did when I was his age, minus my buck teeth. Dane was wiry and small. He lived in Graceville, Florida, but his kin were from Chanute, Kansas, originally. He was very interested in this World Series because Kansas City was playing the Mets.

"Hey," said Dane. "Dewey told me your dad was from Kansas."

I shrugged, but didn't answer. I wished Dane would disappear. I didn't particularly want to talk about this.

"Mine are from Chanute," said Dane. "Where was your dad from?"

"I'm trying to listen to the game," I said.

It was one of the only World Series matchups that I had little interest in. I hadn't wanted Kansas City to make it to the playoffs. I had wanted anyone else to be playing. But you can't control baseball. On that night I wasn't sure who I was rooting for. I don't care for New York. And at the time, I would've rather had my toenails plucked out than root for Kansas.

The game was a heated battle. This was game five. If the Mets won, the series would go to game six. If the Royals won it, they would be world champions.

"My dad used to take me to a lotta Royals games when I was a kid," said Dane.

"Mazel tov," I said.

I didn't give a wooden nickel about what his perfect daddy did with him.

"My folks are from Neosho County," he said. "That's where I was born, but my parents lived in Iola, before we moved to Chanute when I was four . . ."

I wanted to place a strip of commercial duct tape over Dane's mouth.

"Yeah," he said. "I love the Royals. What about your dad? Did he like the Royals?"

"My mother's family's in Georgia," I said. "They're the only family I know. Now would you let me listen to the damn game?"

It obviously hurt his feelings, and I felt bad about this, but there are some areas of life I didn't talk about. Not with him, not with anyone.

Even though he was being quiet now, the damage was done. My mind wandered far from the ball game, into the faded memories of a world I have all but forgotten. I could almost remember Iola, with the colorful storefronts downtown—only a few miles from my father's hometown. And Neosho County. I sort of remembered that too.

The Neosho River, a loping stream that cut through the place my father was born. It was the river where he taught me to gut a fish. I was a kindergartener, far too young to be holding a knife, but he was tipsy at the time. I cut my palm to the bone, blood went everywhere, and I can hardly remember anything else. But I do remember ending up in the Neosho Regional Medical Center.

The funny thing is, if you had asked me to subpoena any of those memories only a few minutes earlier that night, I would not have been able to even find them.

What was wrong with me? And this kid, Dane, where did he come from? Why was he here? And *how* did Kansas City make it to the World Series? They were the worst team in baseball. This was a divine joke being played on me.

Still, if I were being honest, something inside me was rooting for my father's team. The more I listened to the game, the more memories came back. Soon the memories were so thick that I had to swat them like gnats.

The Royals made a stunning double-play. Everyone howled with joy.

Dane wanted to high-five me. I pretended I didn't see his hand.

"What's the matter?" asked Dane. "Aren't you rooting for your dad's team?"

"No," I said. "I want the Mets to win."

It was a blatant lie. I was starting to hope Kansas won.

That's when the restaurant manager appeared at the back door. He was a large man with a red face and a loud voice.

He hollered, "Hey, I got customers inside! Where's my band? If y'all don't get in there right now, I ain't gonna pay you, and you can consider this gig done!"

We found ourselves in an ethical dilemma.

Since there were no TVs broadcasting the game inside, and *since* there were only three customers in the joint, and *since* these loyal customers were mostly old men with hearing aids who wouldn't know the difference between a fiddle and a nuclear explosion, and *since* it was the most pivotal game in baseball, we subjected our final decision to a democratic vote.

When the due process was over, our unanimous decision was to tell the large manager kindly that we quit.

After we broke the news, the manager made a few remarks that were less than Baptist-approved, and we left the parking lot. We drove across town to the sports bar in a caravan of ugly cars with instruments in the backseats. Dane's shift was over so he rode with me. He sat in my passenger seat and would not stop talking. The kid had diarrhea of the mouth.

"You know," he said, "I just went back to Chanute last month. It was awesome. I got to ride my uncle's horses and stuff . . ."

"That's great." I turned the volume of the radio up.

". . . and we went fishing almost every day. You know, there are tons of places to go fishing in Southeastern Kansas."

I pointed to the radio dial. "Do you mind? It's kinda hard to listen to the game with you talking."

". . . and I was shooting dove with my grandpa, and it was awesome. There were so many dove in those fields, man. I'm pretty good with a gun. Hey, maybe we should go dove hunting sometime . . ."

"I'm vegetarian."

"I've never known any vegetarians, but I've known plenty of Seventh-day Adventists, and once when I was . . ."

When I arrived in the parking lot, I shut off the truck engine and hopped out. Dane was following me, talking a blue streak.

"And there was this one time," he went on, "when I was with my grandpa, and we were going to . . ."

Well, I'm embarrassed to say that I was not very nice to Dane. I'd had enough. I turned around and shouted:

"I DON'T CARE ABOUT YOUR GRANDPA OR YOUR HAPPY LITTLE KANSAS FAMILY! JUST SHUT UP! SHUT UP! SHUT UP! SHUT UP!"

I felt worse than I've felt in a long time for behaving that way. It was like I was on autopilot. I'd lost control of myself. Things were coming out of my mouth that I couldn't stop.

"Listen," I said. "Let's just go inside and watch the game, okay?"

He nodded, and I don't know why that kid didn't turn away and run from such a jerk like me. But he didn't. Instead, he asked, "What about Ellie Mae?"

"What about her?" I said. "She's sleeping in the truck."

"But we need her. This is the World Series."

"She'll be fine."

"We can't leave her. She's kinda like your mascot. How do you expect Kansas to win without her? It's bad luck."

I couldn't have felt like a bigger heel. This kid was worried about my dog even after I'd blown up at him. I felt like I'd just shot Saint Francis of Assisi.

Dane ran to my vehicle and returned with Ellie Mae on a leash.

"That's a bad idea, Dane," I said. "They're never gonna let us inside with her."

"Just watch me," he said.

When we got to the door, Dane walked Ellie into the place like there was no problem. And when the waitress came to the table, Dane told her Ellie was his service dog. Dane explained to her that he could not see out of his right eye because of a birth defect. Not only did she believe him, but she brought Dane a free order of chili fries and gave him her number.

"See?" he said. "I told ya."

It was a night to remember. It was the night that four band

members, one fifteen-year-old, and one colossal jerkface with daddy issues watched the game.

At the beginning of the sixth inning, I went to the bathroom. I washed my hands and looked in the mirror. I wasn't sure what I was going through. My first instinct was to take my dog and leave for home. I didn't want to see Dane. I didn't want to see any more of the game. I wanted to drive off and never come back. But the mirror betrayed me. The way the light was hitting my reflection was eerie. It made me look like a carbon copy of a man I once knew. And I missed that man.

When I got back to our table, I could hardly carry on a conversation; my mind was elsewhere. When I looked at the television, I saw the blue-and-white uniforms that my father used to hold so dear when he was alive. Never has a man loved baseball as much as John Dietrich. Never. I could see his lanky frame in the wheat field outside Humboldt. He was pitching to his cousin, and I was sitting on his truck hood, idolizing him.

Kansas scored in the eighth inning. The place went nuts. A man at the end of the bar shouted so loud it sounded like he strained an abdominal muscle.

Kansas scored again. Everyone started hollering, and the air got hot with testosterone. A man wearing a camouflage cap threw his hat across the room, and it smacked another man who weighed as much as a Sherman tank. They were escorted outside to cool off.

The Royals hit a triple. They scored again. It sounded like the room was going to be blown apart. And it was in the ninth inning, after a demonstration of superior pitching by Wade Davis, Kansas City became World Series champs.

The bar turned upside down. Men were shouting. People were clapping. I leapt upward and without thinking threw my arms around Dane, and we jumped up and down together like we'd been friends all our lives. He screamed. I screamed. And

I didn't even realize I was crying. Hard. Our jumping stopped. Dane held me and patted my back.

This drew a lot of strange looks from people in the place. Members of my band surrounded me. Soon it was a six-person hug—not including the dog.

"Hey," Dane said, frowning. "I thought you were pulling for the Mets."

I held the young man by the shoulders and looked into his young face. "Dane, I'm sorry I yelled at you."

"It's okay. Don't even give it another thought."

"You sure?"

"I'm sure."

After our conversation, Dane wandered away from our table. I saw him remove a cellphone from his pocket. He exited the building, holding the phone to one ear, plugging the other. Before he exited, I heard him shout into the phone, "Daddy! We won! We won!"

The universe was screwing with me, that's what was happening. I wished it would have just left me alone. I had to pull the truck onto the shoulder on the way home because my eyes had become too blurry.

It was a quiet night, and the big bay in the distance was looking right at me. I stepped out of my truck and sat on the water's edge.

"We won, Daddy," I said. "We won."

CHAPTER 28

FORGETTING TO FORGET

 The sun was low over the marshlands of the Choctawhatchee Bay. The sky was bright, with purple clouds. The bay was a mirror beneath, reflecting heaven back at itself.

At sundown, our world comes alive, all nature feeds upon itself. The algae gets eaten by the mullet, the mullet get eaten by the redfish, the redfish get eaten by the pelicans, the pelicans get eaten by the chipmunks. No, I'm only kidding; I don't know what eats the pelicans. The brown pelican is a beautiful creature. You can see them dive-bomb the water, beaks first, resurfacing with fish, swallowing them whole.

The sailboats were moored for the night, with stern-lights glowing. A trawler was in the distance, out for shrimp, and dragging for garbage. A small bass boat carried the silhouettes of a father and a son, rocketing across the water at thirty miles per hour.

And a group of people sang "Happy Birthday" to the hardest working woman I've ever met, my mother.

Our voices reverberated across the bay. We sounded like a bunch of Labradors with chest colds. She blushed. She hid her face. But she liked it.

My mother wore her hair back, with her face fixed, and her nice dress on. She opened a few gifts. When she got to my gift, she ripped the paper and then placed her hand over her mouth. Her eyes were reddish, and her cheeks got flush. She swallowed back tears. People became quiet, waiting for her to tell them what she was looking at.

"What is it?" said my sister.

"Is *this* what I think it is?" Mama said.

My mother reached into the box and removed a glass-framed picture. Matted inside was a newspaper cutout. A column written by her son. One of my first ever published. It was entitled "Mama."

"Oh my . . ." Mama said. It was all she said. And it was enough for me.

The column wasn't much, only 482 words, but it was written about her, and for her. I'd been writing for the last few years. Words had sort of overtaken my life.

In the frame was a thumbnail picture of me, embedded beside the column. My face was wearing what photographers like to call an "authorly pose." In this pose, an author sits before a camera, raises one eyebrow, and stares at the lens like a tiger. It's the same look movie villains use just before they say, "It appears you have a talent for *not* dying, Mister Bond."

My mother touched the glass. "You look so serious in this picture."

"It's called an authorly pose," I told her.

"Are you eating enough green vegetables, dear?"

"I paid a lot of money for that photo."

"Can you get your money back?"

Then she read a few paragraphs to herself. Her eyes roamed my words, printed in soy-based ink, on a piece of gray newsprint. Oh, it was quite a feeling to see my words on that paper. My mother placed a palm on the frame. There were veins showing through the old skin on her hands. I had never noticed how much older she was becoming.

Those hands were the same that were once stained with the kind of ink beneath the glass.

"Oh my Lord," she said. "You did it."

"Well," I said. "We did it."

She touched my cheek. "You've gotta sign this for me, sweetie."

"Sign it? Don't be ridiculous, Mama."

"Do it for me. I want everyone to know that my son wrote this, you know, when you're famous one day."

"Aw c'mon, Mama."

That woman has always believed in me too much. Still, it was her birthday, and you don't argue with a birthday girl.

I signed it with a Sharpie and presented it back to her. She kissed me on the forehead, and I could smell her unique fragrance. My mother has always had her own smell. A sweet smell. I can close my eyes right now and conjure up that scent without trying.

Long ago, when she would get home after working a night shift, I would stumble out of bed to greet her. "Seany, what're you doing up so late?" she would ask, holding me against her chest, kissing my cheek. And I would breathe her inward.

I remember holding her on the day of my father's funeral. She was bandaged and stitched. She had every right to spit on his memorial, but instead she was soft and kind. And when we held each other. That smell.

And in the mornings, when we would awake to toss newspapers, and she would guzzle coffee that was strong enough to power residential lawn mowers, she would hug both me and my sister together before we left the house. A three-person hug. That smell was ever present.

"What a gift," she said. "My son, the *writer*. I can see it now. One day you'll have your *own column*."

"Don't be silly."

"You hush. It could happen."

My mother's birthday was beautiful. I ate many oysters that night. My sister danced with her husband on the dance floor. My wife and I don't dance, but we can do the Macarena. My mother and I laughed a lot—something we had gone years without doing. I've never felt like a richer man.

The house band started playing "Rest Your Love on Me," Conway Twitty's masterpiece, released the year I was born. Don't ask me how I know that.

My mother placed her arm around me and we danced. She said, "I remember when you wrote your first book report in the third grade, on that old portable typewriter I gave you. Do you remember that typewriter?"

"Yeah," I said.

"Oh, you were so little. You got a B, I think, and your daddy was so mad at that teacher. He said, 'I oughta go give that woman a piece of my mind.' But he never did."

The band's music filled the silence that passed between us. We swayed in rhythm; my mother was not as agile as she'd once been.

"Oh, he was so proud of you," she went on. "He was waving that book report around on the jobsite and telling all his friends, 'My boy's gonna be a writer!' Did you know that? He said that to all his friends. I don't think I ever told you that."

"No, you didn't."

"He always thought you'd turn out to be either a writer or a musician."

"Really?"

"Oh, yeah. He always used to say, 'My boy's so talented, he's gonna grow up to be a writer or maybe a musician—or maybe even a preacher.'"

Two out of three ain't bad.

Anyway, I'd never entertained the idea that my father would be proud of me or have any faith in me. Not once. I certainly never knew that he believed I would become something respectable. How could he have known these things when I hadn't even known them about myself? If anyone but my mother had been the one to tell me this, I would've laughed.

"He would be so proud of you," my mother said. "Maybe one day, you'll even write his story."

"I don't think so, Mama."

"You never knew him the way I did, and you never knew the sweet man he could be before he . . . before he got sick. Promise me you'll write about him one day. Do it for him, and do it for me."

"Mama."

"Promise me."

"I promise."

"You make me proud to be a mother, Sean."

"I've never felt prouder to be your son. Happy birthday, Mama."

CHAPTER 29

SEAN OF THE SOUTH

 I started a blog on a whim. It's funny how one miniature decision can change a man's life forever. That's what
the blog did for me. My first piece of published writing
gave me the wherewithal to do even more quasi-insane things—
namely, to start an online column.

Life would never go back to normal thereafter.

Before the blog's kickoff, my friend suggested I draw upon
my Southern roots and name it *Sean of the South*, after the hit
Alabama song, "Song of the South." The other option was *Sean
with the Wind*. But everyone agreed the first name had a better
ring to it. So I named the blog *Sean of the South*, pressed the
"Enter" button, and that was the beginning of a new life.

I suppose that some of the greatest things in life happen by
accident. The first entry into my blog was about fishing with my
cousin. It was a funny story—or at least it was supposed to be
funny. I wrote the first draft on a typewriter and rewrote it on
the computer. Then I posted it online.

The next morning I awoke to discover that 400 people had
read it. I almost choked on my coffee. Which 400 people? We
didn't even have 400 folks in our little church.

My next story was a comical tale about visiting my aunt in

North Carolina, about growing up in the shadow of too many women in one house. The next morning, 690 people had read it.

After that, I wrote a story about one of my dogs. And 1,400 people read it. I wrote a few about my wife, several about my mother, and I wrote about the adventures of my old truck.

Then on one sunny summer day, I walked into a Winn-Dixie to buy some ground beef in the meat department. Ahead of me in line was a group of Hispanic boys, maybe fourteen years old, dressed in work clothes, covered in dust. The butcher saw them, smiled, and placed several pounds of beef on the counter. He winked at the boys. "On the house," he told them. "I gotta get rid of this meat anyhow. It expires today."

The boys were obviously stunned. They almost couldn't get words out. One kid seemed to be on the verge of tears.

"*God bless joo, sir,*" said one boy.

"*Jess,*" said another boy. "*Dios te bendiga.*"

It was something that stuck with me. I was so moved that I wrote about it that night. It was a short column, only 460 words, and it took a full day to write, rewrite, and rewrite again a hundred more times until I could quote it by memory.

One hour after I published the story, it had been read 2,000 times. After 3 hours, 15,000 times. The next morning, 220,000 times. My email inbox was filled with hundreds of letters from people I had never met. One man had even written from as far away as Saskatchewan, Canada. At the time, I didn't even know how to spell *Saskatchewan*. In fact, I had to look it up just now.

It wasn't long before the blog became the most important thing I ever did. In a little under a year, people in town had already quit referring to me by my Christian name and started calling me Sean of the South.

After a few years, the title of the blog became synonymous with my name, and it's how people introduced me at, say, bar mitzvahs. Today, even my family, friends, and professional acquaintances sometimes call me Sean of the South. As well as my aunts, uncles, cousins, in-laws, various members of the IRS, and Jehovah's Witnesses.

When I am in trouble at home, my wife will shout "SEAN OF THE SOUTH!" in all caps while holding a chef's knife in the air. This is especially true when I leave the toilet seat up or load the dishwasher wrong.

One day, they will probably engrave this name on my gravestone, and well, I wouldn't mind that. For this title is not just a name to me; it is the symbol of my rebirth. Samuel Clemens, William Porter, and Marion Robert Morrison had their public names. I have mine too, I guess.

Soon I started getting invited to write about all sorts of things of local interest. And after three years, I was covering the most paramount items of journalistic interest in our area. For example: I covered bingo night at the Shady Oaks nursing home, a cattle auction in Chipley, Florida, the Walton County Fair, the Dothan Peanut Festival, the Waverly Tomato Festival, the Brewton Blueberry Festival, the Blountstown Goat Festival, the Wausau Possum Festival, the Baldwin County Strawberry Festival, the Russellville Watermelon Festival, the Opp Rattlesnake Rodeo, the community rummage sale at the Methodist church, Miss Wanda Ann's ninety-ninth birthday, hundreds of potluck socials, basketball games, football games, and, of course, all the baseball I could stand.

My love for baseball was alive and well, and still is. And it's one of my favorite things to write about. This was the first time in my journalistic career—if you can call it that—that I was actually writing about America's pastime. I get excited just telling you about it.

Perhaps my favorite baseball assignment was writing about the Baptist men's softball team. Though, I use the word "team" with affection. This was a collection of white-haired men who all had AARP cards and got senior discounts at the post office.

Most of the athletes had cataracts. Others were victims of severe hearing loss. So half the players couldn't see, the other half couldn't hear, and everyone wore Velcro shoes.

These were men who had no business playing organized sports. And this is why it was so much fun to write about, because there is nothing like watching men seriously injure themselves for the sake of a cork-and-twine ball and pride. A man doesn't age much in his mind, only in his joints and muscles. Sometimes he forgets that he's aged at all because even though he's so old he creaks, upstairs he's Montgomery Clift.

The Baptist men's softball team gathered together a few times per week during the summers to test the limits of their artificial knees and to remember what it felt like to be young. And by George, I wrote about it.

Games would always go the same way. Once the pitcher threw the ball, most men took a while before they actually realized a pitch had been thrown. Often the brain-impulse to swing the bat wouldn't even occur to them until the following morning. But it didn't matter, most who struck out stole first base anyway. The rules were very flexible.

These games were not strict. Once, I saw Mister James Wannamaker hit an infield single, and instead of heading for first base, he jogged straight over the pitcher's mound and collided with Mister Barry Adams, the second baseman. You simply could not have a bad time at these games. These men were so happy they were on fire. And it was infectious.

They were easy to write about. They played the game with heart, free from the watchful eyes of their wives. Each man, no matter his class, ethnicity, or views on predestination, was granted the pleasure of holding a bat.

I had only ever written about their games but never

participated, until the old men asked me to be an umpire one week. That Sunday after church, Mister James chased me in the parking lot. I tried to outrun him, but I was no match for his new titanium hip.

"Sean of the South!" he shouted, trotting after me. It sounds an awful lot like a cuss word when it's yelled like that.

"Hold on, buddy!" he hollered. "I have a proposition for you!"

I started running. I didn't know what he was going to ask, but I knew two things about him: (1) he was Baptist, and (2) he wasn't afraid to ask anyone to volunteer to work in the nursery, even inanimate objects.

He finally reached me. He caught his breath and said, "We need an umpire for the Father's Day game. You'd be perfect for the job, what do you say?"

"I've never umpired before," I said. "I don't think you'd want me."

"C'mon, it'll be fun. You know we always have fun at our games." He rested his hand on my shoulder. "It's either that, or I'll ask you to volunteer in the nursery again."

"The last time I worked in the nursery, I caught hand, foot, and mouth from Molly Albertson, only I didn't *contract* it in my hands, feet, or my mouth."

"Really? Where'd you get it?"

"This is a PG-rated book, Mister Wannamaker."

The truth is, I had a deep respect for Mister Wannamaker. Long ago, when I was a boy, he had taken me to the Methodist church camp for a father-son retreat. He did this because I had no father, and he couldn't bear the idea of a kid like me being alone. That night, at the Methodist campfire, several boys without fathers, like me, were given special treatment. That retreat weekend, he spent more time with me than his own son. You don't forget people like that.

So I agreed.

"Great," said James. "I knew I could guilt-trip you into it if I tried hard enough."

He laughed and gave me a hug. "You'll wanna stop by Roger Springfield's house before the game, and he'll fill you in on the details."

"What details?"

"You know, he'll teach you how to call the game the way we normally call it."

"You mean how to look the other way when someone steals first?"

"You're a smart kid, Sean of the South. I don't care what they say about you."

That evening, I went to Roger Springfield's house to borrow his chest protector, face mask, and pitch counter. Roger Springfield was the team's usual umpire. He had broken his ribs and was placed on strict bed rest. He was a big, loud, happy, boastful seventy-five-year-old who was in better shape than Charles Atlas—and didn't mind telling you about it.

Roger could bench press more than an eighteen-year-old, and even in the dead of winter, he sported an impressive suntan.

Roger's wife greeted me at the door. Then she gave me jars of homemade preserves in a basket, lined with checkered cloth.

"What's this for?" I asked.

"For filling in for Roger," she said. "It means the world to him. This team is his baby, you know. They're scuppernong preserves. Do you like scuppernongs?"

"Like 'em? I would bathe in scuppernongs if the weather was right."

"I just made them a few days ago. Here's another jar for your mother. How is she?"

"She's good."

"And here's another jar for your sister. How is your sister?"

"She's great. I'll tell them you asked about them."

There was a notecard on one jelly jar with my name on it. It was enough to bring a tear to a glass eye. God bless church ladies. A white-haired church woman, I'm convinced, is the fruit of all that is good within America. They are saints who wander the earth largely unnoticed, who know their way around a stove and how to bless the hearts of mankind. They can change a diaper with one hand, skillet-fry chicken with the other, and make a pound cake with their feet.

She led me inside. I found Roger lying on a sofa, watching ESPN at an ear-splitting volume. His white hair was thick. His skin was bronze. His shirt was off, and his big torso was wrapped in bandages.

"Sean," he said in a loud voice. "How're you doing, my boy?"

"I'm good," I said.

"I really appreciate you filling in for me at the Father's Day game. Are you excited?"

I shrugged. "Mister Roger, I don't know if I'm much of an umpire."

"What?" He laughed to himself. "Well, you're a *man*, ain't you?"

"Allegedly."

"You're *breathing*, ain't you?"

"On weekends."

"You're the man for the job."

Roger and I couldn't have been more different. In his living room, I was struck with the realization that this man was like my father had been. He was the kind who, when he hugged you on Sunday mornings, smacked your back so hard you coughed up tiny pieces of your own bronchial matter.

"Have a seat, Sean of the South," he said. "Let's talk about umping. You ever done any?"

"You can just call me Sean, and no, I've never umpired before."

"So you've never swept the dish?"

"How's that?"

"The *plate*, son, the *plate*. Have you ever umped a game at all? Like backyard baseball or Little League?"

"No, but I've played a lot of ball."

"Good, good. What position did you play?"

"Left guard."

"Guard? In baseball?"

"I sat on the left side of the bench, guarding the watercooler."

Thus my training began. Roger turned off his television, positioned me in the center of his den. He dressed me in heavy, oversized umpire gear and cleats. I stood poised, holding a plastic pitch counter in my right hand.

"Okay," he said. "The *first* rule of umping is to keep your shoes polished and your pants pressed sharp."

"What's that got to do with anything?"

"Son, if you don't take your appearance seriously, nobody will have faith in your calls. And the second rule: never smile on a ball field. You're not there to enjoy the game. You're a servant of the people. You don't want to be liked. You want to be trusted by the athletes."

Athletes? Let's be honest here. Most members of the team wore Life Alert bracelets.

Still, Roger showed me how to stand behind the catcher, how to call strikes and balls, how to identify checked swings, and how to judge the strike zone on a lefty.

And most important, Roger showed me how to "pound the cellar door" with my fists when calling a strike.

This is a time-honored umpiring move that I have always wanted to do but never had the courage. It is the most fun an umpire will ever have. Entire games hinge on doing this move correctly.

Roger demonstrated: he hurled his fist forward and pulled his elbow back. "*HEEEE-Rike!*" he shouted.

"See?" he said. "You gotta give it all you got. Now you try."

"Strike," I said in a whisper barely audible by most members of the rodent family.

He slapped his own forehead. "No, from your *gut*, say it loud enough so all the fans in the stands can hear you."

It was a nice thought, but there were no stands at the community ball park, and there certainly were no fans either. We had lawn chairs, and they were mostly filled with paramedics on standby.

"This is baseball," said Roger. "An American game. Show some heart, Sean!"

"*Heee-rike*," I shouted.

"Louder!"

"*Heeeeee-riiike!*"

"Blow the roof off my house!"

So I reached into my belly and pulled out the biggest sound I could: "*HEEEEEEE-RIIIIIIKE THREEEE! YOU'RE OUTTA THERE, BATTER!*"

"That was pretty good," Roger said. "There's hope for you yet."

All that yelling and pounding cellars made my bladder weak. I had to use the bathroom. Roger told me where it was. When I walked through his hallway, still wearing my chest protector and facemask, I passed an open door that caught my attention. The room was an office filled with trophies, ribbons, plaques, signed baseballs, autographed footballs, and photographs on the walls.

In most of the framed black-and-whites pictures, a young Roger dangled from a steel building, wearing a hardhat.

That's when I felt pain, just beneath my chest protector. I thought about my father, the steelworker, the baseball player, the loud talker. What he would be doing if he were still alive and seventy-five years old? Would he be playing softball, or at least umpiring games like Roger? Probably so.

My father, like Roger, was all the things I never became. I had hardly any of his qualities. He was a workaholic, an exceptional sportsman, and he could tell stories that tore a group of men apart with laughter. I was a thinker, a procrastinator, a sleep-until-eleven-thirty kind of guy, and kid who had a preference for typewriters.

On one section of Roger's office wall I saw photos of him jogging in a race. The young version of him wore a look of exertion on his face, his clothes covered in sweat. His legs were pillars. His shoulders were broad. He was running a rock-covered trail, sloped downward. There was blood on his jersey, and there were cuts on his face.

Roger's voice came from behind me. "Oh yeah, that was one incredible race."

"It looks like it."

"I was forty, a long, long time ago. That was my tenth marathon, hardest one I ever ran. I fell four or five times on the downward descent."

"*Downward* descent?" I said.

"Yeah," he said. "The marathon has an *upward* ascent. It was tough too, but nobody ever told me that it's even *harder* coming back down the mountain. Fourteen thousand feet above sea level, it could kill you. You fall on rocks, get cut up, and you either keep going or just lie on the ground losing water, oxygen, and blood—either way you could die. It's really a lotta fun."

"Sounds great."

"Oh, but it's so beautiful up there. I worked as a steelworker all my life, stood on top fifteen-story buildings, but nothing is like that marathon."

"I didn't know you were a steelworker."

"Union man. I apprenticed when I was nineteen."

Beside photographs of a man dressed in denim, wearing a

toolbelt, was a framed T-shirt. On the yellow shirt was an illustration of a mountain. The shirt read: "Pikes Peak Marathon."

I experienced a brief jolt, like someone had left the window open. This was Pikes Peak Marathon. A race on my father's mountain. He had been at 14,115 feet above the earth for a long time. He'd been rained upon, snowed upon, tossed in the wind. He had seeped into the soil so that the calcium from his bones had become the very pH in the dirt, eventually sprouting into greenery that became food for wildlife. He was a piece of that mountain now. In a way, he was in every picture, every drawing, and upon the sole of every foot that touched the mountain.

"I go once every few years just to hike it. Can't run it no more, but I can still move my legs."

Roger opened a photo album. He rifled through more photos of mountains.

"In the morning," Roger said, "if you're lucky enough to see a sunrise, it's like nothing you ever seen in your life. Last time I was there, there were people painting, you know, with oil paints. It's pretty inspiring. I think even you'd find something to write about up there. You really ought to go sometime."

I thanked him for the umpire lessons and showed myself to the door.

That Father's Day, I called my first game as an umpire. The game was against the Methodist team, affectionately known as the "Water Sprinklers," and the Baptist team, the "Billy Graham Crusaders." Baptists lost, 39–1. Then I wrote about it.

And even though a big-city editor once remarked that "nobody wants to read stories that are about elderly people and happy things," an average man named Sean Dietrich wrote them anyway.

CHAPTER 30

ELLIE MAE

Nobody in their right mind decides to *do* public speaking. Myself included. To become a public speaker, you have to go to diction school. There, a woman will fill your mouth with marbles and teach you to talk around the marbles. Each week, she removes two marbles. Once you've lost all your marbles, you're ready for public speaking.

It was a Monday morning. I stood on a stage holding nothing but a microphone and all that remained of my dignity. There were six hundred people staring back at me in a high school gymnasium. Six hundred.

These were students, teachers, football players, cheerleaders, librarians, and one principal.

Whenever I spoke into the microphone, my voice would echo through the gymnasium until it sounded like an auditory hallucination.

"Hello, my name is Sean . . ." I would say.

What I would hear was:

"*Hellomynameismyseanhellomynameisseanhellomynameissean hellomynameisseanhellomynameismyseanhellomynameissean . . .*"

I was dying on the vine. My collar felt tight. I cleared my throat over the mic, and the cheap speakers rang with feedback that sounded like the Starship Enterprise about to land on the roof. The PE teacher raced to the soundboard and adjusted the volume.

"Someone kill me, please," I was thinking. "Kill me now."

I was not designed for public speaking. My whole life, I've been the quiet kid. The kid voted most likely to collect stamps. The kid who had a hard time answering without stammering.

"I should've never agreed to this," I thought to myself. "What in the Sam Hill was I thinking?"

The school had asked me to deliver a talk to a bunch of students who read my blog regularly. I had denied the request several times, but they persisted. Finally, I'd agreed to do it, and I realized I'd made a big mistake.

Six hundred faces were looking at me like I had roaches crawling out of my ear holes. My worst fear has always been looking foolish in front of high schoolers.

"It's good to be here today . . ." I went on.

"*Goodtobeheretodaygoodtobeheretodaygoodtobeheretodaygood tobeheretodaygoodtobeheretodaygoodtobeheretoday . . .*"

Come, Lord Jesus, come.

I reminded myself to breathe. I was not feeling well. This was probably a panic attack. I was sweating, my stomach was aching, and my ears were ringing. I was not programmed for huge crowds. The doctor once told me I had a syndrome called *vasovagal syncope*. It's a harmless condition, but it means that whenever you get really worked up, you pass out. No warning signs, no nothing. You just up and fall over.

I have passed out a lot during stressful moments, usually at doctors' or dentists' offices. It has also happened in a few restaurants—mostly at expensive restaurants when the waiter hands me the bill. Also, it happens whenever I see snakes, poisonous spiders, poison ivy, clowns, bad TV shows, or anything written by Danielle Steel. On one occasion, I passed out after

I totaled my truck. When I awoke, the paramedics were standing around me, snapping their fingers, shining penlights into my eyes.

"Tell us your name," said one paramedic.

"My what?" I said.

"Tell me what your name is. I need to hear you say it, sir, or I can't let you go home."

"My name is Sean Dietrich."

"Middle name?"

"Danger."

Behind him, I could see my pickup truck in the distance, crumpled like the bellows of my granddaddy's Weltmeister accordion.

"Will I be okay?" I asked.

"Oh sure," he said. "You just passed out from shock is all. We call it *vasovagal syncope*. Lotta people have that. You're really lucky though, Mister Dietrich. Most people poop their pants, but you didn't."

"How about that."

I only hoped I would be so fortunate when I passed out before these six hundred teenagers.

My speech was interrupted by howling. Then, from the back of the high school gymnasium, I saw high school students start to murmur and point at something. A few stood to their feet, others were laughing.

"Oh my God," I thought. "It's happening. This is how I will die. I will fall over right here, in a high school gymnasium, bump my head on the floor, break my neck, and die. Please, Lord, if I die, don't let me poop my pants."

But the students weren't giggling at me. They were cackling at something from the back of the auditorium. Soon I saw what they were pointing at: a large, hulking, overgrown, uncoordinated, ninety-pound, floppy-eared, drooling, smelly, black-and-tan bloodhound. And she was running straight toward me.

My wife had been holding Ellie Mae on a leash in the back, but Ellie considered leashes to be minor challenges. She was dragging my wife forward. My wife was stumbling, shouting, "ELLIE MAE! NO!"

The kids were going hysterical. Ellie had that effect on people. Finally, Ellie Mae had broken free from my wife and ran through the auditorium like Free Willy. She weaved through rows of kids, bestowing her drool upon them, offering blessings to all who touched the hem of her collar.

"Ellie Mae," I said in a scolding voice over the microphone. "*Elliemaeelliemaeelliemaeelliemaeelliemaeelliemaeelliemae elliemaeelliemaeelliemaeelliemaeelliemaeelliemae . . .*"

Ellie ran through the audience. She loped with the clumsy running style that all bloodhounds have. It's more of a forward leap than a run. She climbed the steps of the stage and jumped on me. The room applauded her. It was a standing ovation. For her encore performance, she licked herself and then chewed on a mic cable.

This dog gave me confidence. I don't know how it happened, or how she did it, but there was something magic about that beautiful animal. My words loosened in my throat, and I felt more relaxed. I started telling stories over the microphone, and I was having a marvelous time. I don't remember what I spoke about that day, but I am certain I did a terrible job. Even so, I did end up having fun.

When we got home that night, after I fed Ellie supper, I checked my email only to discover that I had four more requests to speak. And thus my entrance into the world of public speaking began.

That year, I spoke for Rotary Club meetings, Kiwanis Club fundraisers, Baptist fellowship halls, fairground jelly contests, library book clubs, church lawn concerts, some funerals, a few weddings, and on one occasion, I delivered a sermon at a Presbyterian church—a day I'd like to forget. Don't get me wrong, I wasn't exactly Dean Martin over the microphone, but the more I spoke, the more I started to realize you can do something you're bad at and still have fun.

After a few times, I started to feel comfortable on stage, telling stories, talking about growing up the way I did. And I was coming to realize something about my fellow man. Everyone has had a hard life. Some have had it harder than others, but all have suffered. And suffering is suffering. And I learned that it unites us, the same way laughter does. I learned that everyone has had a difficult childhood. Everyone has felt alone at one time or another. Everyone has once felt the same way I felt.

I came to understand that I was not alone and never had been.

Furthermore, I realized that people didn't want to hear about sadness when you had a microphone in your hands. People had enough heartache of their own within daily life. People wanted to be cheered up. They wanted to hear the words of someone who was happy. They wanted to laugh. They wanted to feel good.

So I started telling stories about my own life. I made them humorous, but the kernel of every story was something I had never told anyone before. I was talking about my mother, my cousins, and about my thirteen-year-old bloodhound. I began telling stories with the intention of making people giggle, or at least smile for a few minutes and feel relief from the abrasions of life. And I started speaking about my father. I told good, happy stories about him, not the dark stories that he left us with.

The more people laughed, the more fun I had, the more relaxed I became on stage, and the more open I became about my life.

Soon, I was telling audiences about all the dirty laundry in my life. My educational failures, my pathetic attempts at finding a career path, and my tough childhood. For the first time I was retelling the stories of my dismal life with a lighthearted voice. And it was becoming clear to me that I could mine for precious metals in the coal mines of my past.

And this is how storytelling saved me. Over the next three years, I found myself speaking four times per week, sometimes more. We traveled to every state in the Southeast. I told simple stories, and tales of growing up without much confidence, and I told people about my father. I talked about him so much that I felt like I knew him again. And the curves of his face were coming back to me.

We spent 80 percent of our life on the road, sleeping in pet-friendly hotel rooms, eating complimentary continental breakfasts, taking Ellie Mae to do her business on hotel lawns.

And one night, while I was walking beneath the stars of Montgomery, with Ellie Mae on a leash and my wife hooked around my left arm, I realized I had a family. My own family. How did this happen? How did a broken kid become a family man? No, we didn't look like other families, but we were happy. And I'm ashamed to say that happiness has always been such an unfamiliar emotion to me, that I almost felt guilty for feeling it sometimes. But not anymore.

For some reason, that one night is burned into my mind. We didn't have much in the way of material possessions. We drove old cars, and at the time, we lived in a twenty-eight-foot trailer home. At night, an elderly bloodhound slept between us on a queen-sized bed, and when it got cold, our toilet didn't work.

But I was happy. I was no longer the young man with the dreary outlook. I was not a construction worker with sore muscles or an ice-cream scooper in a pink apron. Not a busboy, not a drywall man, not a bar musician. I was a writer and a storyteller. My God.

Somehow I had finally fallen into my place in the giant jig-saw puzzle.

I hugged my wife and my dog that night and told them both how much I loved them. Ellie licked my face; my wife kissed me in a dry spot. And I was the luckiest man in the county.

A few mornings later, I left for Birmingham for a speaking engagement. I kissed my wife and my bloodhound goodbye, I packed the truck, and I left our little home in the woods for the rural highways between Walton County and the Magic City. I would only be gone a few days.

I drove away that morning feeling just about as glad as I'd ever felt, seeing my wife and my dog in the rearview mirror. I'd be hard pressed to recall a time when I felt any better. I sang with the radio. I rolled the window down and let my arm hang out.

But good things, I have learned, are not meant to last. If they did, we might never understand how beautiful they really are. If a flower lived forever, it wouldn't be something we admire, I guess.

When I reached Maplesville, Alabama, my phone rang. It was my wife. She was crying on the other end of the line. Her voice was serious.

"Sean?" she said. "I'm at the vet. You might want to pull over the truck. It's about Ellie Mae."

I veered to the shoulder of the highway, and it was the worst day of our lives.

CHAPTER 31

THE FUNERAL

Ellie Mae Dietrich died of acute pancreatitis, and I had never felt the sting of pain I felt over her passing. Not even for my father. I never let myself mourn my father the way I allowed myself to mourn my elderly bloodhound, who I referred to as "my daughter."

The night Ellie Mae left us, I collapsed and cried into the floor of my hotel room until there was a puddle beneath me.

Somehow, I had to give a speech that night, but I don't remember anything about it. I didn't sleep for days, and when I awoke during the nights, I could swear I heard a dog snoring. But when I looked around the room, she was not there. Our bed was empty. Our home felt like a tomb.

I know what you're thinking. She was just a dog.

No. Ellie Mae was more than a dog. She was some-*one*. She was one of the greatest females to ever live, though she was not human. Ninety pounds of lanky legs and loose skin, and a tall, beautiful tail that never failed to give away her true feelings.

She was all animal, and something more. Her senses were finely tuned. Not just her nose and ears. Her heart was every bit as alert as her nose. She could read minds, and that's not speculation—it's fact. She was the only dog I ever knew who could decipher the thoughts of a man and gauge what he would do next. Within a few moments of an introduction, Ellie Mae could read your fortune. She could sense your personality. She could smell your kindness, sincerity, or happiness. She could sense a man's dishonesty, self-centeredness, or ill intentions.

She was closer to this earth than most people are. And therefore, part of it. She lived with her bare feet touching ground. In the summers, she cooled herself by sleeping on it, wallowing in the mud if need be. And maybe it was because of this that she seemed to know more about life than I did. Maybe this is why she could smell things in the air you didn't know were there. Like emotions and exciting ideas.

Sadness within a person brought out the mother in her. She could console me in a complete way because she knew nothing of our human boundaries. She would lick, snuggle, wallow, and bite you tenderly.

She felt joy more than humans could feel it, because she did not restrain for the sake of being civilized like people do.

Anger was an emotion altogether foreign to her. She laid her head to rest every night without resentment.

My grandfather used to say that once in every man's life, he would receive an example of the divine. Once and only once. It would be tangible proof that would remove all doubt and change a man's mind forever if he paid attention to it.

Abraham got his proof from the sky, Moses saw a flaming bush, the writer of the hymn "How Great Thou Art" found proof in nature, and my proof came from a ninety-pound bloodhound.

I know it sounds grandiose, but inside, she was more than animal. When she slept, you could almost see it in her face. Something else was in there. Something bigger. Maybe if you would've removed Ellie from her earthly body, just for a moment, you would've seen her spirit. Maybe it was a giant bright light, strong and brave, the size of a city like Los Angeles, hovering above the petty, entangled lives of man, watching over the boy she was sent to love.

You would've seen that her wingspan was large enough to stretch from Tallahassee to Huntsville. And you would've heard singing from her brothers and sisters, from all her ancestors. And you would've taken a knee and said, "My God, how great thou art."

In the weeks after she died, I kept her ashes in a cedar box on my truck dashboard. She went with me wherever I went, riding in my cab the way she always did.

At night, I would hold her remains in my lap the same way I did with a man I once knew. And I would think about her. I would close my eyes and feel my own hot tears on my cheeks. And I would imagine her, running across a wide open prairie, toward water. Always water.

One night, in my mind's eye, I could see a large tree in the distance, a live oak with large limbs and a trunk that was bigger than a Buick. A man stood beneath it. He was tall, lean. And he was calling this dog. The man patted his legs. I could hear his two-fingered whistle in the distance.

The black dog ran toward him. And it was as though she knew him. They rolled in the grass together, and I could hear sounds of distant laughter. She didn't judge him for his sins. She held none of his mistakes against him. Dogs never do.

They were so far away from me, the man and the dog. They were only moving dots on an imaginary horizon, but it hurt me to know they were together, and I wasn't with them. All of a sudden, it hurt that my father had been so far away for my entire life, not because he was in an eternal home but because I'd kept him there and never brought him any closer.

That night, I wiped my face. I sniffed my nose. I conjured up all the braveness I could. I walked inside our trailer home, Ellie's remains beneath my arm, and I placed her on the mantle.

"Are you okay?" my wife asked.

"I'm going to visit my father," I said.

CHAPTER 32

ON THE ROAD AGAIN

A few days after Ellie Mae died, a friend told me about a farmer in Molino, Florida, who had a litter of black-and-tan bloodhound puppies. On a Sunday afternoon, my wife and I drove to Molino to hold them. That's all we wanted to do. We needed to hold a dog and smell puppy breath.

When I met the runt of the litter, I smelled her breath. She bit my nose and drew blood, and I knew that this dog would never ride in anyone else's truck but mine. We called her Thelma Lou. She chewed everything. And anything she couldn't chew, she peed on. The dog had at least three accidents per minute. Sometimes more.

I tossed a baseball for her. She ran after it in the clumsy way bloodhounds do. She ran back to me, carrying the ball in her mouth.

It was morning. I had been awake since before sunrise. I couldn't sleep because it was an important day. I felt a mixture of thrill and uneasiness. I'd been counting down the hours until we left to visit my father's prairie and his mountain. And the morning had finally arrived.

We would be tearing across the South and the Midwest and into the Rocky Mountains of the West. I was not the young man

I used to be. I felt ready. Though, in some ways, I felt more like an infant than ever before.

When the sun rose, so did my wife. And it was time to load the truck. Before we departed, I adjusted the side mirrors. I took a few breaths. I don't know why I was so nervous, but I was.

"You ready?" my wife asked, touching my forearm. "I know how hard this must be."

Truth be told, I wasn't sure if I was entirely prepared. How does a man know if he's ready? After all, I'd thought I had been ready years ago. I'd gone westward only to be met with a silo of stored resentment and bitterness.

"I don't know," I said. "Am I?"

"You are."

"How do you know?"

"Because you have us with you."

I glanced in the rearview mirror. In the backseat of the vehicle was a lanky Thelma Lou. Her legs were the size of telephone poles, and her head had already become so heavy she couldn't stand upright without falling forward. She was eating a pillow.

I fired the engine. I was a captain, about to ride the turbulent seas of his own past. I was a cowboy, about to make a ride from the South to the West. I was a sojourner. A pilgrim. The hero of my own movie. I was looking for any metaphor to make it easier. I drove our gravel driveway very slowly.

And before we exited town, my wife turned to me with love and understanding in her eyes and said, "Thelma Lou just peed on the seat."

CHAPTER 33

YOU'RE DOING IT

"You're doing it." I said to myself. "You're really doing it this time. Don't chicken out. You can do it, big guy."

That's what I mumbled beneath my breath. I often talk to myself in the car. Sometimes, I talk to myself in public too. For example, in supermarkets I might mutter something like, "Where did they move the coffee?"

I do this because the supermarket authorities are always reorganizing the grocery store for no discernible reason. One day, you might walk into your supermarket and discover that the coffee aisle has been replaced with the back-to-school-supplies-and-cans-of-pumpkin-on-clearance aisle.

During these important supermarket visits, if I *don't* talk to myself, my mind will wander—just like it did when I told you about the cans of pumpkin. Then I get distracted and forget all about coffee and end up coming home with the ingredients for cheesecake. This attention deficit disorder makes life hard, especially when you are, say, writing a book about your life.

The drive was beautiful enough to make a grown man weep. When you pass through Alabama and catch your first glimpse of sunlight spreading itself on acres of unruly wiregrass, it makes you melt inside.

You see the old fence posts made from crooked limbs that sacrificed themselves a hundred years ago. You pass serene cattle, standing near the highway, counting cars. Tall longleaf pines swallowed by kudzu. Shallow creek bridges with bicycles parked nearby.

There are rusted trailer homes with fancy cars out front. And fancy trailer homes with rusted cars out front. I am in love with trailer homes because every member of my family, extended family, and most of my friends have lived in one at one time or another.

Dogs wander the highway shoulders—no collars. Kids walk the side of the road—no shirts. Remnants of old chimneys still erect stand in acres that have gone to weed. Shotgun houses with sofas on porches. Dog-trot houses with families of twelve inside.

Truck stops near the interstate, loaded with eighteen-wheelers. Billboards reading, "Jesus is coming," or "Get right, or get left," or my personal favorite on the Autauga County line, "Go to church or the devil will get you." It doesn't get any more fundamentalist than that.

After ten hours of highways leading to more highways, you are getting sleepy. Two lanes become three lanes in some places. The solid double line goes from being dotted, to solid, to dotted again. The reflectors in the center of the road look like twinkling orange stars in the night, outlining the curvature of hills and the deadly hairpin turns.

You stop at gas stations, long after the world has gone to bed, and you need strong coffee. The attendants behind the counter, working the night shift, are red-eyed and sluggish, and look at you with weary faces. You are in Oklahoma now, heading toward Kansas. You turned back, years ago, in this very part of the Panhandle. You wonder if you have the guts to keep going.

You tell the cashier, "The card reader on the pump doesn't

work." He only shrugs. He looks like he just turned twelve. He's not going to do anything about the card reader. So you pay cash.

And while you're filling up your tank beneath the midnight blackness, you see a family in a minivan at the pump beside you. Their doors are open while Daddy is at the pump. Their plates are Kansas plates. It hurts a little bit.

Children are sleeping in the minivan's backseat. They are wearing Kansas City Royals T-shirts. You're getting closer to your father's home state, the place where it all went haywire. It's a place you've blocked from memory, so that when you actually *try* to remember it, all you find is a black hole.

But you've been through this before. This time, you're ready for the ugly feelings.

You focus on pumping gas. The filling station sits across from a wheat field. It goes on for miles in the dark. God. It's been a hundred years since you've seen an actual wheat field. Something inside you remembers fields like this, but you're not sure how.

And you're driving again. The roads are lit with headlights and stars. You are hypnotized by the sounds of your own wheels. You see license plates that read "Arkansas," "Missouri," and a few "Kansas" tags.

The farther you drive, the farther you are from your home. Or are you getting *closer* to home? What is *home*, anyway? Is home the place you were born, or somewhere else? Why are you so confused about things that are so simple for other people?

People ask your wife where she's from, and she has a simple answer: "Brewton, Alabama." When people ask where you're from, you have a ten-minute-long explanation. You say, "Florida," but then you explain how you got to Florida by way of Atlanta. All the while, you are wondering where you belong. You're thinking about the tragedy that was your early life, and how your father's family excommunicated you. They didn't want you. The Kansans didn't want you. And because of this, you never knew them. But it wasn't their fault. Suicide doesn't just kill one person. It wipes out families.

These are the reasons why you can't tell where home really is. Wherever home is, it isn't on the plains. This place is foreign. Or is it? No matter what anyone says, you can't change biology. And right now, while driving, you feel your father's lineage getting closer. You feel it in this soil. You smell it in the dry air.

The closer you get to Kansas, the more you realize that you never knew this place. This makes you sad.

Trucks pass you in the left-hand lane and make sounds like a small hurricane. The tail lights of other vehicles are sparse red dots in the distance. Maybe they're warning signals, telling you to turn back. Maybe you're doing the wrong thing coming this way. Maybe you should just go somewhere fun with your wife and your puppy and forget about pilgrimages.

"No," you say aloud. "I've come this far, and I'm gonna keep going."

It's getting late, and you're getting so tired that you're starting to worry you'll fall asleep behind the wheel. So you sip so much black coffee that your kidneys are shutting down.

You are about to cross the Kansas border. God. Why did you do this? Why? You foolish kid. Go back home. What are you hoping to see? The memory of a man who tried to turn your family into a headline? Are you nuts? He doesn't deserve you. You've made a mistake coming this far. Leave. Go. Now.

You pull over again. You roll into a truck stop to refuel and breathe the night air. You are still talking to yourself, encouraging yourself.

"Oklahoma," a sign reads over the front doors of the convenience store. You buy some peanuts and a Coca-Cola.

The cashier looks at you and says, "Where're you from?"

That question.

"Florida," you say. "I think . . ."

The cashier looks at you funny. "You *think*?"

Stupid boy.

You pile into your truck, sip more coffee. Your dog and wife are asleep in back. You are an hour away from Ground Zero. The small town where you were supposed to begin your life—before a madman with a rifle changed the course of history. Before your mother left the ugly state forever. You barely recall it, but you remember that when she crossed over the Kansas line, bound for Georgia, she swore she would never come back to this "godforsaken hellhole again." That's what she called it. And your evangelical mother never talked like that.

You remember how she used to talk to herself while driving, mumbling beneath her breath, trying to give herself courage.

"Drive," you say to yourself. "Just drive."

In the distance, your high beams hit the large blue state sign.

"Now Entering Kansas," it says.

"Oh my God." That's what you say aloud.

The sign is tall, located within a million acres of spring wheat. You veer to the shoulder. You have to get out. You don't know why. You have to see the Vietnam battlefield.

The gravel beneath your heels makes crunching sounds. You are overcome with exhaustion and emotion and hesitation and fear. A lot of fear. But you stand beneath a night sky and wonder about the things that made you, you. What are you?

More driving. You don't need the map anymore. Kansas is divided in a gridwork of square miles that are simple to navigate, and you don't care where you're going now; you're here and that's enough.

Folks in this state are so rural they have to mail-order sunshine. You can feel that. You pass prairies that hold the blood of your ancestors who fought in the Civil War. Some were Confederates. Some were Union men. They were farmers,

cowboys, pilgrims, plow hands, German immigrants, and aboli-
tionists who bled for what they believed.

You drive past towns that have all but dried up and vacant
service stations with rusted farm equipment out front.

Now you are in the wastelands of the Sunflower State, alone
with your thoughts. Orange sunlight appears behind you. It's a
sunrise over the Kansas plains, and the sight stuns you. It's not
that it's beautiful. There is something about it that pricks a hole
in the darkness of your memory. The veil that hides the things
you thought were forgotten is beginning to fall. And you begin
to see things inside your head that you forgot were there.

A tall, skinny, redheaded man, holding you on his shoulders. Camp Creek, winding into a thicket, and you, catching
crawfish. The Kill Creek downtown, with a bar, a library, a post
office, a small Baptist church. A heron, staring at you.

Sunrise. A sky is painted with purple and orange smudges.
You lull past Pittsburg, Cherokee, Beulah, Greenbush, Erie,
Earlton, and you have to stop. You have nothing left in your
energy stores. But you keep going because it feels good and bad
at the same time, the most confusing sensation you've ever felt.

Your body will pay for this all-night drive, of course. You're
not as young as you used to be. You're a grown man with a back
surgery under his belt. You're tired and feeling middle-aged.

The truck pulls to the side of the road, almost on its own.
You're just going to close your eyes for a few minutes. That's all.

Instead, you spend the last bit of your energy on tears. Inside,
you know that you are only a few miles from a place where your
father was baptized, where he played baseball, where he ran
through the water spill-off beneath the water tower as a boy,
where he would bale hay, where you were conceived. And it hurts.

You adjust your seat backward and watch the sunlight
spread itself on the acres of unruly wiregrass, the way it did in
Alabama, hours earlier.

You see old fence posts made from crooked limbs of old trees. And the serene cattle stand near the highway, counting cars.

It almost feels like home, except it's not. Home is not a place on a map. Home is not a one-word answer. Home is this woman, sleeping in your passenger seat, and the animal who sleeps behind you. Home is a feeling. And an idea you have to fight to preserve because this world tries to take it from you.

"You're doing it this time," you tell yourself. "You're really doing it, don't be afraid, you can do it."

You close your eyes but open them now and again. When you do, you see the long golden prairies that you had almost forgotten.

"Don't chicken out," you mumble.

But you are chickening out. You don't want to be here. You want to turn around, head south or west or east or anywhere else but onward. But you keep talking to yourself.

"You can do this," you say. "You can do it."

And you say this to yourself until you fall asleep.

CHAPTER 34

HUMBOLDT BEGINNINGS

 Humboldt, Kansas, caught the noon light like a catcher's mitt, and it could not have looked more like Mayberry, USA. Downtown features an old-style water tower, a few brick storefronts, a cafe, a police station, nine churches. It's not just beautiful—it's forever lost in time.

I grew up hating Kansas. Even the combination of letters that form the word itself were revolting to me. But here in the town square of my father's youth, I was having a change of heart.

The quaint town of Humboldt is home to the world's largest Bible parade. Actually, it's the only biblical parade in America. It's been going since the early sixties. People come from as far away as Wichita to see it. Folks lines the streets and have more scriptural-based fun than you can shake a stick at.

There are pony rides, beans and hocks, gospel quartets who sing until they pull a muscle. You can hear Pentecostal preaching, high school marching bands, and of course, see the parade.

On the main drag, the magnificent evangelical display rolls by. There's a float for every book of the Bible. Everyone's favorite float, as I understand, is Jonah and the Whale, which features a forty-foot papier-mâché whale on a flatbed trailer cruising by spectators with its mouth open. In the jaws of the great fish are a pair of moving bare legs that belong to an actual, real-life Baptist.

Humboldt is the kind of place most people wish they grew up in. It's a community so tight it squeaks.

I wandered into a cafe and sat. My wife sat across from me. The waitress who came to the table spoke with a thick accent that was vaguely familiar to me.

"What'll it be, darlin'?" she said.

I asked if the woman knew any Dietrichs. Her face lit up. "Dadgum! I knowed you looked familiar. You kin to the Dietrichs?"

"Yes, ma'am."

"You know, I graduated with Pat."

"Is that right?" I had no idea who Pat was or whether Pat was male or female.

We left the restaurant and drove the rural dusty roads. I saw the place where my father was born. There was no wooden structure anymore. It was just an empty field with a crushed clapboard house and cattle roaming beside a barbed wire fence. I stepped out and tried to imagine a farmstead, a barn, and chicken houses.

I was numb inside. Not because I didn't feel anything but because I felt too much at once. It was almost like grabbing a hot skillet that just came out of the oven. The millisecond after you touch the handle, right before the burn sets it, you feel a numbness. Within this moment, your mind doesn't fully realize what happened. But after the cool numbness subsides, the burn is fully felt. Then you have no choice but to feel it.

This was it. This was the place.

My father was born right here on September 11, 1953. It was a good year for America. Gas was twenty cents per gallon. Dwight D. Eisenhower was the new president. Ernest Hemingway won a Pulitzer for *The Old Man and the Sea*. Marilyn Monroe was in Hollywood, singing about diamonds. The Brooklyn Dodgers were on fire. And in this field, a redhead came into the world, hundreds of miles from civilization.

He grew up to be a radio fanatic from the beginning. He liked to listen to ball games and old radio shows like *The Lone Ranger, Six Shooter, Lum and Abner, Your Hit Parade*, the *Grand Ole Opry*, and *The Jack Benny Show*.

I can recall entire evenings spent in his lap, listening to his old Philco radio. He'd bought the radio in Iola at a department store when he was twelve. He kept it his entire adult life, and it was a well-loved machine. It was his escape from a terse family and abusive people. He carried that radio the same way other children might have carried a teddy bear or a blankie.

I drove the rural paths to see Humboldt's hayfields, wheat fields, and livestock pastures. They were wide, and long enough to resemble the acres found in heaven. The land seems to run toward the edge of the world and spill right over into oblivion, uninterrupted by tree lines or mountains.

The Kansas sky is so wide that you can lie on your back in a freshly scalped field and see nothing but blue from east to west. I'm not sure how I even know this. But I do.

If you lie on your back on a cloudless day, the blueness will start to disorient you and make you dizzy. This is my father's world. Kansas was his state. Humboldt was his cradle.

I drove each street twice. I touched the brick Catholic church on Central Street where he was first baptized, before he was rebaptized as a lifelong evangelical. The chapel still stands and is hardly big enough to play a game of ping-pong inside of. The Baptist church is still on Seventh Street. The Methodist church still sits two streets over.

He went to a school on New York Street. Back then, my father once told me, school let out early so children could help their families in the fields or with the cattle. Here, education was not at the top of the priority list. The list was: God, family, farming, and baseball. Education was a distant fifth.

There were no theaters, no drive-ins, no nothing. The town rolled in the sidewalks at eight o'clock.

While the rest of the world was enjoying the modern amenities of the 1950s, this rural town was still marveling at electric refrigerators. They were light years behind the rest of America. Their telephones were still wooden boxes with cranks, mouthpieces, and handheld receivers. My father said once that he could remember ice delivery trucks rolling along, the ice block seated in a truck-bed of sawdust. Who knows if that's true.

In his day, air conditioning was a myth. Nobody had ever seen one, and few had ever felt one. The nearest television was two hours away by car in Emporia. Radio was king.

My father had a troubled childhood. His mother was Swiss German with six children and a drunk for a husband. She was tall, lean, and angry. She used her hands to get her messages across. His father was also thick-handed and strong. And when he drank, he was a fury.

As a boy, my father saw his parents fight in the kitchen. His father would slap his mother until she was either out cold or huddled in the corner, begging him to stop. My father was so afraid at night, he would lie in his bed too scared to crawl out and use the bathroom. So he would hold his bladder or his bowels until he wet or soiled his bed.

His father was a man with hands like hams, a thirty-inch neck, and a tuft of red hair on his head. He was loud, funny, jovial, handsome, solid, and he could handle more liquor than a whiskey barrel. He was built for farming, steelworking, tinkering on cars. He used his hands—for everything.

My daddy once told me he was only five years old the first time his father smacked him. His father hit him so hard it knocked him off his feet, and he knocked my father's head against a chair. Daddy got used to being hit.

So did his mother. My father's father beat his mother so often he'd broken her cheekbones. Once, his father hit her so hard he knocked out most of her teeth. She wore false teeth until the day she died.

My father was plagued with ulcers as a child. He had a nervous stomach for the rest of his life, and he was a notorious hypochondriac. And it's not hard for me to see why. However, depression was his biggest cross to bear. Periods of melancholy during adolescence became so bad that he had been committed to a "home" for a short period when he started to have a nervous breakdown. He wouldn't have wanted me to tell you that. But I think you deserve to know it after reading this far.

Daddy tried to take his own life at least twice in his youth. Those are only the times anyone knows about. Once when he was fifteen, he locked himself in his parents' car, parked in the garage, engine running, garage doors shut. The exhaust filled the place and made him sleepy before someone found him. Another time, when he was sixteen, he tried to shoot himself with a handgun. Someone found him before he went through with it.

He found solace in baseball, and in radio. He told me he would curl up in his childhood bedroom with his radio in his lap, listening to Westerns, or Minnie Pearl, or Bud Abbott and Lou Costello, or gospel music coming out of a station in Iola on Thursday nights. He loved gospel music. Maybe because it was hopeful.

In his adulthood, my father would get so depressed that he would curl up into a corner and stay there for forty-eight hours. My mother would find him and beg him to get up. But he would only cry or stare into a wall until he was no longer in his body.

When my mother would try to pull him out of his hole, he would look at her and say, "Leave me alone. I don't wanna live anymore."

The first time my father hit my mother, he bruised her so badly she had to call in sick to work. She should have left him then, I know. She was a vibrant young woman who had more brains than ought to be allowed. But she was also a tender woman, too trusting, and at times—forgive me, Lord—naive.

My mother has always believed in second chances. And it is here where her power lies. I would not be the person I am if my mother had not been so forgiving. She has extended mercy toward me a million and five times throughout my life. She granted the same courtesy to my father, even when he did not deserve it. Even though he used it against her.

I remember the first time my father hit me. Like him, I was five years old. He smacked me only once. I stumbled backward. It stunned me. I can still hear the sound. It was a loud thud in my head. I don't even remember what I did to provoke him.

What I do remember was that after he hit me, his face changed. He wore a look of horror. Then he held his hands before him to observe them, and he started crying.

"I-I-I didn't mean to do that," he said, weeping. "What have I done? My God, what have I done?"

He reached for me, but I ran from him. He chased me. He caught me. I covered myself. But he only held me close in his arms and sobbed like a child. His tears fell on my shoulder.

"I didn't mean it," he said. "I didn't mean to do that—please forgive me."

Later that same night, he came into my room while I was asleep. I saw his dark shape in the doorway. He sat on the edge of my bed and rubbed my hair. His hand was warm. And he smelled like beer and cigarettes.

He spoke in a whisper.

"I made a promise to myself when I was a boy. I swore I'd never lay a hand on my child, if God ever saw fit to gimme one."

I heard him sniff. I heard him heave.

"My daddy was a hateful man," he went on. "First time he hit me . . . well, I remember it. You never forget something like that."

No, you never do.

My father was violent, almost against his will. Once, when I was a boy, my father taught me to drive his Ford tractor. A red-belly tractor with a gray hood. I lost control of the wheel and ran it into a sycamore tree. It smashed the grill of the great machine, and it made a loud boom.

My father saw it from far off. He marched toward me. He gripped me by the collar and flung me to the ground. I hit the dirt so hard I had a mouthful of dust. He smacked me. I ran from him. He caught me. He threw me again. He smacked me again. He stood over me, and his look terrified me.

He was not himself. He was another man. I don't know who, but it wasn't him. This man had big eyes and clenched teeth.

I outran him to the house and found my mother standing in the kitchen. She placed me behind her own skirt and stood with wide legs, hands balled into fists. I'd never seen her stand so firm.

"You touch him again," she said, "and it'll be the last thing you ever do."

"Move out of the way," he said.

"I'll kill you, dammit," she said. "Or I'll die trying."

I hid behind the folds of my mother's dress.

Daddy took one step toward her; she took one step toward him.

And I truly believe my mother would've killed him graveyard dead if he had tried anything.

Eventually, my father returned to his senses. And that same night, I found him curled in a ball, lying beside that dented tractor. A radio was playing a ball game in the background. He was bawling, with his face pressed into a work blanket. I crawled beside him. He held me tight, kissed me on my hair, and said something I'll never forget.

"I don't know who I am."

You learn to endure people who torment you. And you learn to live through it, I guess.

I don't want you to misunderstand me. He wasn't a bad man. He was a good man. And beautiful. But like I said, you never forget some things.

The last time I saw Humboldt, we had celebrated his birthday. We drove to Allen County to see his uncle Lawrence and aunt Delpha. My father took me around town to show me the landscape. It was a place he loved. I don't think I've ever seen him so happy as he was that night. He was fully himself, and he was beautiful. And when Daddy was happy, everyone was happy. Even the trees and the grass were happy. I fell asleep in his arms, listening to a small Philco radio while he snored. Happy moments are only meant to last for a little while.

He shot himself three days thereafter. And I would hate this place after that. I had promised to hate it forever.

But now, looking at these wide blue skies, I wondered if I'd lied.

CHAPTER 35

OUR HOUSE

 A long gravel driveway led to the two-story farmhouse, which was yellow. I don't remember it being yellow. Was it yellow when I was a boy? No, it was gray. Or maybe it was white. Shouldn't a fella be able to remember the color of his own childhood home?

"Here it is," I told my wife.

She held my hand tightly.

It moved closer to us. I started to feel ill. The dilapidated farmhouse had shutters that were crooked and falling off. The roof was covered in muck. It was never a pretty house, but then again, most farmhouses aren't. Still, I remember it was attractive when I was a child.

Not anymore. There were weeds everywhere, rusted farm implements in the front pasture, an overturned boat with a rotten hull, overgrown with poison ivy. The chicken coops, the goat pens, the small barns, the sheet-metal sheds—they had all seen better days.

"I wonder if anyone's home," said my wife.

"I don't know."

I saw nobody around. I wasn't even sure anyone lived in the house anymore.

I walked the property calling out, "Hello? Hello? Anybody home?"

I rounded the corners of the front porch. I knocked on the back screen door.

Someone had to live here. There were animals everywhere. Goats, llamas, cattle in a distant pasture. Chickens roamed the yard freely. I had always thought chickens were evil creatures. We raised them when we lived here.

As a boy, I would wander into the coop, and they would peer downward at me from their roosts with lifeless doll eyes.

I could feel my knees shaking. The sound of wind, sweeping across the woods, along the prairie. It was like hearing an old song.

I was greeted by a white Leghorn chicken that leapt into the air, fluttering its wings, and landed with her talons against my chest. I caught her and held her. After I got over the shock of it, I realized she was friendly. So I stroked her head. And I named her Gertrude.

"Gertrude?" asked my wife. "Why Gertrude?"

Why not Gertrude?

I walked the old homestead with Gertrude in my arms and touched nothing. I only looked. I walked toward the back fence where my father and I used to sing to the cows once upon a time. I saw the mighty trees he planted one summer with a handheld spade. They were saplings then, when he dug their holes, no taller than my knees. Now they had trunks that were big enough for an eight-year-old to climb.

Gertrude and I walked through the scraggly woods, beneath the canopy of green until we reached Camp Creek.

My breath caught in my throat. The old water looked good, but it was much bigger than I remembered it. The water was moving quickly and making white foam against the rocks on the shoreline. I sat on the shallow concrete bridge, legs dangling, petting a chicken, and I remembered too much at once.

Catching mudbugs in a plastic bucket. Hooking catfish with

a trotline. Hunting squirrel, rabbit, and coons with a twenty-two. Gigging frogs with a long fork and a headlamp. And I saw a boy laughing in the distance. He had a friend with him. They were splashing through the creek, shouting to one another in excitable voices.

"Hey!" the boy shouted. "I got one! I got one!"

"Where? Where?"

"Over here!"

Gertrude was docile, but she got fussy when she heard the shouting. Apparently the shouting wasn't imaginary. It was real. There were *real* boys in the creek water. One child in the distance looked at me. He lifted his hand in greeting.

I lifted mine.

We sat for nearly an hour. Then, without warning, Gertrude leapt from my arms and fluttered into the sky. She hit the ground and started high-stepping toward the house again. I don't know why, but I stood and followed her.

The chicken wandered through the tall grass, making a path for herself, going God knows where. Finally, she arrived at a gnarled tree, and then she stopped and started pecking the dirt around the exposed roots.

It took me a few moments to realize what I was looking at. The tree was tall, with a wide trunk. On its branch was a tire swing, dangling from an orange-and-white rope that was nearly severed from age. The tire was gray from years of sunlight and dry rotted. It moved slightly in the breeze, like it was alive. I felt my whole life come back to me.

I stepped toward the swing, but Gertrude cut me off. She jumped into my arms again. She clucked. It was as though she were telling me, "Look, but don't touch."

The high limbs of the tree were fat and sturdy. The leaves were so thick that they blocked out the sun and glowed lime green before the light.

A lifetime ago, I saw a steelworker climb this very tree. He held a rope between his teeth and scaled the trunk with ease. I watched him shimmy outward onto a long branch and tie a bowline knot. All the time, talking to the child below, who watched him as though he were a superhero.

In many ways he was. I know that you probably have a hard time loving my father after some of the things I told you. But that's only because you didn't know him. Once, he was beautiful.

We'd lost him forever. But then, we had lost almost everything. All the things that were around me. The house, the land, the creek, our family, and everything that was in the state of his birth. We lost our identity, our pride. I lost myself.

The swing was still here.

I don't know why this moved me so much. But it did. It was evidence of something. Evidence that he loved me, maybe.

Gertrude and I loped toward the house again. "Hello?" I shouted into the air.

Nothing.

I stood before the two-story house, holding Gertrude against my chest. I saw my old bedroom window, curtains drawn. I stepped onto the old porch. I overlooked a world of wheat and thistle and meadowlarks.

I saw tiny shapes in the sky, dark dots poised against the sunlight. I heard their quacking when they made their final descent on the distant creek water.

"So," I said to Gertrude. "You come here often?"

The small flock of mallards landed on the water and started swimming in tight circles like they had business there. This made me smile, and if I'm not mistaken, even Gertrude grinned. My eyes roamed the shore of the old pond where I used to catch bream and white crappie. And I took it all in. The cattails, the algae, the low trees, the lily pads.

My eyes stopped when I saw a tall shape in the brush. I saw the S-shaped neck and the long beak. It was a heron beneath the shade of a tree, surveying gray water. He stood amid tall grass, a stately bird with slow movements, a relaxed posture, and control. He looked across the pond at the ducks, and I waited for him to turn his eyes to me. I just knew he would. But he never did. Sometimes you don't get what you want.

It's better that he didn't. He looked happy right where he was.

I bid Gertrude goodbye, placed her on the ground, and thanked her for being my guide. She walked away, clucking. Then I whispered goodbye to the heron. But when I looked for him, he was no longer there.

CHAPTER 36

PURPLE MOUNTAINS MAJESTIES

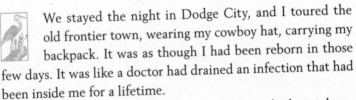

We stayed the night in Dodge City, and I toured the old frontier town, wearing my cowboy hat, carrying my backpack. It was as though I had been reborn in those few days. It was like a doctor had drained an infection that had been inside me for a lifetime.

The world seemed virgin to me, like it had just been unwrapped and handed to me. I was a Southerner stuck in the Midwest, a million miles from the Panhandle, but loving my life.

We hit all the tourist spots in Dodge. I got my picture taken beside the town sign, and we ate lunch downtown. My wife and I went to dinner and a show—a recreation of the television show *Gunsmoke*. I was a foreigner in my father's country, and there is something thrilling about anonymity.

When we got back to our hotel elevator, I noticed the couple in the elevator was staring at me. This made me self-conscious. When the elevator stopped at my floor, the doors slid open, and I started to step out of the elevator car. Before I finished my step, the woman said, "Excuse me, sir?"

I turned around and held the door. She was staring at me. She was older, with white hair and pearls.

"You're gonna think this is weird," she said, "but are you Sean Dietrich?"

You could have knocked me over with a paperclip. I was 1,100 miles away from home, in the Old West.

"Did my wife put you up to this?" was all I could say.

"No, are you *him*?"

"I am."

She slapped her husband. "I told you it was him."

He removed a phone from his pocket. "Do you mind if we get our picture made with you?" he asked. "We read your blog every day. We're from South Carolina."

I couldn't have been more surprised if I had woken up with my head stuck in the refrigerator. I felt sorry for these people because my eyes were starting to feel hot and wet. I draped my arm over the Carolinian couple while her husband held a phone outward to take four or five selfies.

All my life, I'd seen Kansas as unfriendly soil, but today it was not.

The woman glanced at the pictures to make sure she looked skinny enough. Then she shook her head and made us take some more. This time she held her camera higher up and slightly tilted. "This is the trick to looking skinny," she said.

"Take the dang picture, Edith," said the man. "My face is starting to cramp."

She snapped roughly ten pictures until she was satisfied.

"So," the husband finally asked. "What brings you all the way out here to Kansas, Sean of the South?"

I was taken off guard, choking back tears.

"I'm visiting an old friend," I said.

When I got back to my hotel room, I sat in silence for a few minutes. All my life, I've been a nobody with a sad story behind him. But today, in Dodge City, I was not seen as anything but a writer. It was redeeming.

We left Dodge early the next morning and crossed into Colorado a few hours later. And when we reached Colorado Springs, it was breathtaking. Literally. I mean I couldn't breathe. I had always thought Colorado to be so beautiful that you could practically hear Morgan Freeman narrating the scenic overlooks as you drove past.

But no voiceover accompanied these panoramas. There was only pain and immense suffering. And I am not talking figurative suffering. I mean the nonallegorical kind. I felt like dookie.

It started to take a toll on my physical appearance. When I saw my face in the rearview mirror, I looked sickly and dehydrated. My eyes were sunken, my cheek bones were visible, my hair was flat, and all my teeth had fallen out.

"What's wrong with me?" I asked my wife.

"They say the altitude is tough to get used to," my wife said. "Gotta be sure to drink plenty of water."

She guzzled a liter of water until the bottle was empty.

"Can I have some of that?" I asked.

"Sorry," she said. "That was the last of it."

"I'm thirsty."

"What's your point?"

"My point is, if we were on an airplane, and the oxygen masks flipped out of the ceiling, would you make sure I was safe before you put yours on?"

"No. The flight attendants *clearly* explain that you're supposed to make sure your *own* mask is secure before you help someone else."

"You'd let me die?"

She shrugged. "If the masks are coming down, we're all probably dying anyway. If you were to die first, I'd say you were pretty lucky."

The first thing you'll see in Colorado are happy tourists. There are dozens of vehicles pulled along the sides of the road at every scenic overlook. Passengers leap from their cars to enjoy the beauty. Various Midwestern families stand beside the guard-rails, arms slung around each other, flashing happy smiles to cameras. We pulled over at one such scenic stop, and I was short of breath before I even got my legs out of the truck. I could not manage a full inhalation, I was dizzy, dehydrated, confused, disoriented, and I kept thinking my name was Herb Alpert.

Colorado Springs is 6,035 feet above sea level, which might not be too bad if you're visiting from Nebraska. But I'm from Florida—I think. My house is ten feet *below* sea level on wet-lands. We are as low as you can get without using a straw to breathe. I felt like a piece of jerky. No matter how much water I drank, I could not hydrate or get rid of a pulsating headache. I was starting to feel confused and found it difficult to speak clearly.

When we arrived at our destination, my wife helped me out of the truck. She escorted me up the porch steps into our rental house.

"Are you gonna be okay?" she asked. "You are acting weird. Have you been drinking enough water?"

I meant to say, "I'll be fine, honey." What came out of my mouth was, "I think I'm dying."

"I think you need to drink more water," she said.

She placed me in bed. But I did not sleep that night. I only flailed from altitude sickness and dehydration. At one point, I awoke to find my wife petting my hair. And I'll never forget what she said.

"Of course I would help you with your oxygen mask. I was only kidding."

CHAPTER 37

CLIMB EVERY MOUNTAIN

The next morning, I awoke and was almost completely over my altitude sickness. I felt the remnant of a headache, but not like the day before. I stepped onto our porch and took a breath of cold air and was greeted by the tallest mountain I've ever seen.

It was your quintessential mountain. Triangular, purple, and snowcapped. Fog covered it like a dishrag. Thelma Lou was sitting beside me, still sleepy.

The sounds of daily life were beginning along the residential street, lined with sycamore trees and sidewalks. People rode bicycles; others walked small dogs. An old man was taking out garbage. A young woman was retrieving her newspaper.

My father loved this place, and I could see why. There are some things that you can't understand when you are a child. It takes adulthood to make them clear. I knew why he loved it here. To a Kansas man, it was nothing like a prairie. It was the Hereafter.

The house we were staying in sat within the shadow of Pikes Peak. I could see the mountain so clearly I could almost see the vehicles rolling up the roads. The mountain was at least fifty times bigger than I remembered.

You expect things in your childhood memory to appear small when you revisit them as adults. That's not always the case. Sometimes it works the other way around.

My coffee mug was warm in my hand. I stared at the soaring rock, so tall it was blueish, stabbing into the mesosphere. Emotions were getting strong.

Within my chest, I carried the same feeling you might get after watching a sad movie. Not the kind of movie that's so sad you never want to see it again, but the sort you watch over and over because it feels nice to cry. The kind with Dolly Parton, Sally Field, and Shirley MacLaine in it.

The sensation started behind my eyes and traveled toward my chest, working its way down my neck and over my shoulders. This was not what I had expected from his mountain. I had expected a bitter sorrow. Or perhaps familiar anger, like the last time I traveled toward him. But none of that happened. There was only the chest-heavy warmth I often feel during the final scenes of *Steel Magnolias*, after Shelby's funeral.

My father was becoming more vivid by the moment. I am not exaggerating when I tell you that I could almost see the man I had forced myself to forget. He was peering over the bannister of Pikes Peak, watching me. He was waving, shouting, "You ought to see the view from up here! C'mon up!"

All traces of his earthly torment were gone. Not some, but all. His skin was not weathered like it had been. It was supple. He was younger and fatter. He had full cheeks, a healthy smile, strong eyes, and a big heart. He was waiting for me.

Without finishing my coffee, I crawled into my truck. I rested my hands on the wheel and took a few steadying breaths. I cranked the engine. I rode through the town at a snail's pace. The mountain stayed in my windshield until it was so close I couldn't see sky behind it.

The ranger at the park gate stopped me. I paid a fifteen-dollar entrance fee, and he gave me free advice in return. "Put your car in first gear on the way down, and whatever you do, don't ride your brakes, not unless you wanna have your name in back of the paper tomorrow."

"Thanks for the tip," I said.

"No," he said. "A *tip* would be telling you to plant your corn early this year. I'm *warning* you. Put your truck in first gear or you could die, partner." He touched his hat brim. "Enjoy the mountain."

I drove a winding road upward. I pulled over at each scenic overlook to admire the quilt work of faded landscape below. The mountain was still ridding itself of morning fog, and when the mist finally lifted, it revealed nothing but majesty.

The higher I climbed, the farther away my own life became. At high altitude, my ears started to ring, and my breathing became labored. My entire past seemed to shrink into nothingness. The good, the bad, the failures. The world and all its memories were thousands of feet beneath me. And I was temporarily suspended from it all, like a bird flying above choppy water, unaffected. It all became tiny and insignificant and covered by miasma.

The closer to the sky I got, the more dreamlike things seemed. Maybe it was the thin air, or the green scenery, or the sound of my own breathing, or the roads that cut into the mountain. My old, worn-out memories were no longer worn. They were fresh and aromatic. Like cinnamon buns. And bacon. I love bacon.

Here, I could revisit them without the amnesia I'd grown up with. No longer was there a black spot in my brain, but clarity. What was this sensation? Was this remembrance? Was this what people saw before they died, when their life flashed before their eyes? I could see everything, from childhood through adulthood.

"So this is where the memories had all gone," I thought to myself.

The memories of farmhouses and tire swings and leghorn chickens and Little League games and old guitars and eating ice cream at Dairy Queen after Wednesday night potlucks and camping trips and fishing canoes and pocket knives and casseroles and my young mother wearing an apron, frying chicken.

I'd been wrong about this mountain. All the sweet memories of my father had turned into vapor and collected themselves on the ceiling of the world. This is where they had been, waiting for me. And now they were all around. Maybe this is what my friend Dewey felt long ago when we visited Tennessee.

When I reached the last overlook, I hopped out of the vehicle and looked at the whole world. And I saw it all. Not the world. Me.

It was like watching film reels. And I smiled so hard my eyes got wet. The corner bedroom at my aunt and uncle's house in Georgia, and the smell of my aunt's cooking. My mother throwing newspapers before sunrise, hurling them from a Nissan window. Her, crying from exhaustion and sadness.

A boy. His little sister. The guitar this boy's mother bought for Christmas for thirty dollars at the thrift store, and the way the broken family sat around the Christmas tree one year, in grief-stricken silence.

And the young man from Humboldt, who my mother once loved. The joke teller. The handsome steelworker. The turbulent, confused, shouting, funny man who could climb any tree with his bare feet.

A man who once came home from work early, when we lived in Spring Hill, Tennessee, to take me to the Grand Ole Opry. A man who gave me rides on his shoulders when I was a toddler.

The in-the-park homerun I hit during the Little League Regional Championship. The way he smiled at me from the back pew when I sang for a chapel full of his peers. The unique laugh my father had that sounded like a horse sneezing. The way he placed me in bed when I pretended to be asleep. The way he smelled. The way he would measure my height on the wall with a pencil, making marks on the plaster.

I had forgotten nothing. I only thought I had.

Before the final leg of my drive upward, I stopped at the gift shop. I wandered inside and bought T-shirts, pins, buttons, commemorative coins, ball caps, bumper stickers, and one over-priced insulated coffee mug that cost $29.99—which is highway robbery.

The oxygen deprivation was beginning to get to me. I had four thousand feet left to climb, my ears were popping, and I started to feel lightheaded.

When I reached the summit, I could hardly hear. My ears were so pressurized it felt like they were going to burst. I pulled into the parking lot and steadied my shaking hands by shoving them into my pockets. I leapt from my truck into thin air that was so still and quiet that it killed all sound. It was sunny weather. The sky was slate blue. The views were grandiose enough to kill a man.

It was still morning. There were few vehicles around me. I was almost totally alone.

The views were everything my father said they were—I could see that now. This was a rare place. Here you could understand how a person could write a song entitled "America the Beautiful." It was here that you actually wrap your mind around the idea of infinity.

I followed a narrow trail that led me over igneous and granitic dirt that has been at 14,115 feet above sea level since the day Adam bit the apple. I walked until I stood before a tall rock. The thing towered above me. I crawled onto it. I admired the view.

I was wrong about everything. My whole life, I've been

wrong about it all. I expected the mountain to bring me to him. But it hadn't. This mountain had brought me to myself.

The child with red hair, who didn't know where he belonged, grew up disappointed, angry, sad, and lonely. Once, he stood on this rock and felt wronged by the universe. He was a kid who once dumped his father's remains from a plastic bag and wished for a miracle that day that he never received. He wanted signs and wonders, like in the Old Testament. He deserved a miracle. But life doesn't work that way.

But that doesn't make life any less reverent. Or sacred. Or magnificent. And I was so enamored by the beauty of it all I could not breathe.

Not the beauty of the mountain, but my own life, peppered with miracles that trickled inward from unseen rivers, though I did not notice them. The miracles hadn't looked like I thought they would. They never crashed like ocean waves. They had been small, quiet rivers.

I saw a cloud. At first, I didn't pay it any mind. It was only a little cloud, about the size of a cotton ball, and only a hundred feet from me. The cloud began to swell. In a few minutes, it became the size of a house. Then it tripled, quadrupled, quintupled in size until it was bigger than a city. Soon it covered the sky until it hid the sun and blotted out the world around me with gray fog.

The sky became filled with a boiling, wave-like formation. And small, white flakes began to land on my shoulders. First a few. Then a dozen. Then truckloads.

Before long, the air had turned white; the blue of summer was gone. The flurries flew in whirlpool shapes that shifted into clouds. You couldn't tell whether snow was falling upward, downward, or sideways.

And it was here, on this rock, where the hot feelings of anger froze forever, the sting of my life finally easing. And for the first time in history, it became a cold day in hell.

I started talking in a quiet voice. Not for his benefit, but for mine.

"Surely goodness and mercy shall follow me all the days of my life. And I will dwell in the house of the Lord. Forever."

And I finally finished a prayer that was started twenty-five years ago.

Amen.

CHAPTER 38

THE SHOWMAN

 The Mount Vernon Theater in Tallassee, Alabama, is an old theater where Hank Williams once performed. It's your typical small-town opera house, with folding seats, wooden ceilings, a ticket booth out front.

There was a bluegrass band playing something fast and bright before I went on stage. There were four hundred people in the audience, clapping in rhythm.

When they finished, I was telling stories.

Storytelling was not a line of work I thought I'd ever find myself in. In fact, I hadn't known storytelling was even an actual job until people started asking me to do it. But then, life is a comedy, I suppose.

During one particular story—the one about my uncle and an infamous Maxwell House can—I noticed an old man in the front row. He was wearing dark glasses. The man smiled like he'd just discovered teeth. This gentleman was always the first to clap and the first to laugh.

On stage, I told the stories about childhood. I told tales of my father and about how he took me to the Grand Ole Opry once. I told stories that I hoped would make people feel good—even if only for a few minutes. The goal of my life is to make people feel good. Anyone. Hopefully even you.

The man in the front row never quit grinning. He gyrated his head in an unusual way when he laughed.

It had been a busy week. Within those particular seven days, I'd been in five different states, doing the same kind of show. I had been telling stories, playing guitar, and singing with a band. I'd been in Florida, Alabama, Georgia, Tennessee, and Kentucky. I was tired, and my eyes were bloodshot. My wife and I had been living in hotels, surviving on gas-station coffee.

When the show finished, there was a reception in a local fellowship hall. People gathered around potluck tables that were placed end to end and covered with tablecloths. The buffet was filled with the usual fare. I ate seconds and thirds.

"You know something?" my wife said to me, while eating chicken and dumplings from a Styrofoam plate. "This is the first home-cooked meal we've had in days."

Our faces were too greasy for kisses on the cheek, so we touched elbows. This woman is everything to me. Without her, my life does not work.

That's when I noticed a man walking toward me. It was the old man in dark glasses. He held the arm of a woman and carried a long white cane. He had no paper plate, only a toothy grin. When he neared me, he stretched his hand outward.

So I pumped his hand. He had a firm grip.

I tried to release it, but he would not release. Instead, he just held it. He only smiled and said, "Your voice got lower since the last time I saw you." He smelled like Old Spice and sweat.

And that was it. Then he walked away, tapping his cane on the ground before him, holding the woman's elbow.

Before I could follow him, a group of women came to hug my neck. They attacked me. The ladies had traveled all the way from Nashville to see the show, and it was one woman's birthday. I tried to keep my eye on the man while I talked with the ladies, but I lost track of him. He disappeared into a sea of heads. Finally I said to the women, "Ladies, I hate to be so rude, but would you excuse me?"

I darted outside. I ran through a full parking lot, weaving through a maze of cars, looking for him. I saw nothing and almost gave up.

I'm glad I didn't, because I saw something in the distance. It was the dome light of a vehicle. I saw the old man and woman crawling into a truck.

"Wait!" I yelled.

I jogged after him until I was out of breath.

"How do you know me?" I asked.

He removed his glasses. His eyes were white. He reached his hand outward to feel for me. He held one of my hands.

"Because you were all he talked about."

"Did you work with him? Did you know him? What's your name?"

He only fuzzed my hair. He replaced his glasses. He crawled into a burgundy truck with a crucifix hanging from the rear-view mirror. The old woman jumped into the driver's seat. She fired the engine. The man asked, "Do you remember what I told you, a long time ago?"

"Yes."

"Good boy," he said.

He waved goodbye. I waved back, though I don't know who I was waving to. I watched tail lights disappear into the night and saw the Kansas plates. I have no idea who that man was or where he came from, but he said a few words to me a long time ago, on the worst day of my life.

And as it turns out, he was right.

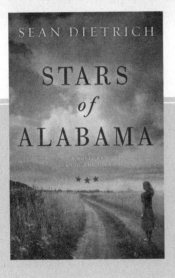